BMW MOTORRAD

A Two-Wheeled Legend

Christopher P. Baker

WHITE STAR PUBLISHERS

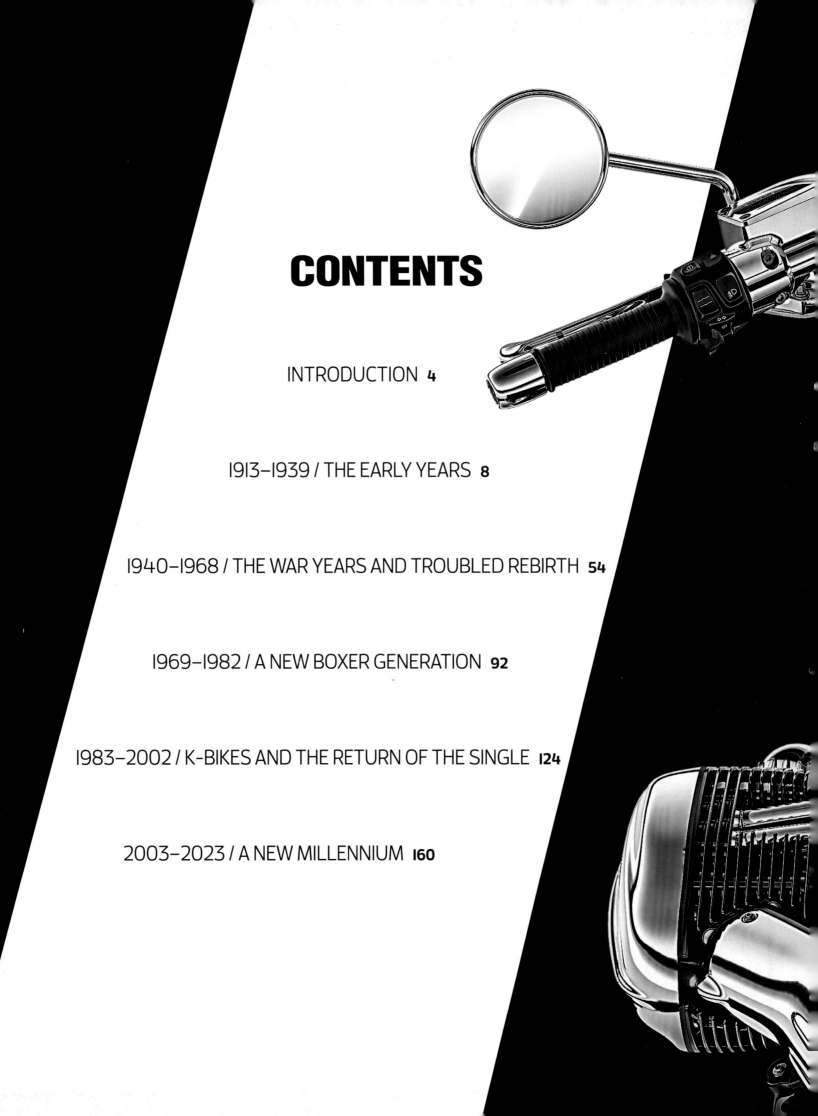

CONTENTS

INTRODUCTION

On average, a new motorcycle rolls off the assembly line at BMW Motorrad's plant in Spandau, on the outskirts of Berlin, every 60 seconds. During peak production times, that's an astonishing 1,000 bikes a day. When Bayerische Motoren Werke (Bavarian Motor Works) celebrates its 100th anniversary of production in 2023, it will have manufactured some three million motorcycles since the company's first machine—the R32 "boxer twin"—was introduced at the Paris Salon in 1923.

In 2021, BMW sold a record 194,261 motorcycles, with the distinctive and classic flat-twin boxer models accounting for around half of the total. From powering the relatively simple yet technologically advanced 494cc R32 of 1923 to the retro-futuristic, state-of-the-art 1,802cc R18 (the highest displacement boxer that BMW has ever built) introduced in 2023 for the company's production centenary, the iconic horizontally opposed twin-cylinder "airhead boxer" engine has become so synonymous with the legendary German marque that no other motorcycle manufacturer has attempted to copy it. In fact, the timeless and versatile boxer became so beloved that it met huge resistance among the company's client base in the 1980s when BMW tried to replace it.

Proving itself (and improved upon) every year, the brand's defining hallmark motor has ever since remained as deliberately close to the original as possible. Of course, BMW has introduced singles (as early as 1925), as well as inline fours and sixes (launched with the K series in 1993) and even four-cylinder transversely mounted engines (with the S and M series sports bikes introduced in 2009). But the amazingly versatile boxer twin has consistently remained at the heart of the company's entire model range to this day.

The iconic "airhead" twin gained a massive boost in popularity in 1980 with the launch of the ground-breaking, dual-purpose R80 G/S (Gelände/Straße) model. Considered to be the world's first true "adventure bike," the G/S proved equally capable on and off the road, and it quickly launched an entire new concept of long-distance adventure travel. BMW has since set the international benchmark in the adventure market, boosted by early top-of-the-podium wins in the Paris-Dakar (the most demanding rally in the world) and by such round-the-world journeys as those of Helge Pedersen, Elspeth Beard, Sam Manicom, and (in 2004) actors Ewan McGregor and Charley Boorman for the BBC's *Long Way Round* TV program.

So successful has BMW's enduro (off-road) segment become that its top-of-the-line G/S and G/S Adventure series today accounts for one-third of the German company's entire annual motorcycle production, with more than 60,000 sold in 2021. Many manufacturers produce faster motorcycles. Most make cheaper bikes. But no other manufacturer can lay claim to combining such consistent practicality, versatility, quality, and reliability as BMW. "The BMW is famous for not giving mechanical problems on the road and that's what he is counting on," recalled Robert Pirsig in *Zen and the Art of Motorcycle Maintenance*, regaling his 1968 across-the-USA road trip with his mechanically fearful friend John Sutherland at a time when BMW motorcycles were still relatively rare in North America. From their inception, BMWs were also significantly more expensive than competing marques, but their premium price was (and remains) justified by their undisputed reputation for quality, reliability, and innovative engineering—traits that have maintained the company as the motorcycle industry's foremost leader.

It's an astonishing success story for a company than began a century ago as a merger between two aircraft engine manufacturers in Munich. (Contrary to popular myth, the BMW badge does *not* represent a spinning propeller; it combines the Bavarian colors of white and blue inside the black ring logo of Rapp Motorenwerke.) BMW's reputation for unparalleled design and build quality owes much to its roots in the precision-conscious aviation industry. Its reputation for also building bikes that are both extremely functional *and* a sheer joy to ride owes much to Bayerische Motoren Werke being situated in the shadow of the Bavarian Alps. Since the outset, BMW motorcycles have excelled in the twisting back roads of the Bavarian countryside and, since the 1930s, the more sporting realm of the German Autobahn.

A seminal evolution came in 1969 with the introduction of the /5 series (500cc R50/5, 600cc R60/5, and 750cc R75/5), using the most significantly updated boxer engine in three decades. The R75/5 could reach 177 km/h (110 mph), still far short of the blistering 200 km/h (125 mph) Honda CB750 and other four-cylinder Japanese motorcycles that had begun to dominate the European and US markets. The 898cc R90S (1973), however, had a top speed of 200 km/h (124 mph), and with its elegant looks (including bikini fairing and sexy airbrush paint scheme) reestablished BMW at the forefront of motorcycling's mainstream after two decades in which the German marque failed to capture the public's imagination.

R90Ss even finished first and second in the first AMA Superbike race at Daytona in 1976 before winning that year's AMA Superbike Championship.

With a four-cylinder, in-line 999cc engine and top speed of 360 km/h (224 mph), BMW's current flagship superbike—the 205hp S1000RR—is leagues apart from the edgy, cool, race-winning R90S. Yet the race-ready, multiple TT winner is merely the latest German wonder machine in BMW's early tradition (since 1925, with the R37) of offering aggressively agile sporting models alongside their more sensible, even plain, workhorse boxer tourers.

The 1983 introduction of the in-line, four-cylinder "flying brick" K bikes vastly broadened BMW's market appeal, adding to the massive boost generated since 1980 by the dual-sport G/S series. In 1993, the airhead boxer engine that had served since 1923 was finally replaced by a state-of-the-art oil-cooled boxer engine (introduced in the R1100RS sports tourer) that further bolstered BMW's sales. By the millennium, BMW's sales in the United States rivaled those of all other European motorcycle manufacturers combined. In Europe, the German marque was firmly preeminent.

Today, BMW Motorrad's remarkably diverse 36-model lineup spans fun roadsters in four engine types; eight adventure bikes (from the BMW G310GS single to the R1250GS Adventure boxer); seven full-bagged tourers, crowned by the ultra-luxurious BMW K1600GTL; seven hypersonic sport and racing superbikes for the absolute philistine thrill; and ten Heritage bikes, highlighted for 2023 by the glamorous, limited edition BMW retro-themed R18 100 Years classic.

Fifty of the most iconic models are profiled in this tribute to a century of BMW excellence.

3 *Glistening with chrome side panels and pinstriped gloss black paint, the R18 100 Years' teardrop fuel tank recalls the iconic R5 of 1936.*

Right *BMW's flagship S1000RR sport bike at sunset.*

1913

1939

THE EARLY YEARS

FROM AIRCRAFT TO MOTORCYCLES

The BMW legend begins in Munich in 1916 with the merger of aircraft manufacturer Otto-Werke and aircraft engine manufacturer Rapp Motorenwerke to create the Bayerische Flugzeugwerke GmbH (Bavarian Airplane Works, or BFW). In 1913, Germany and Austria were preparing for conflict with the Entente Powers and had placed a large order with Rapp for aircraft engines. Karl Friedrich Rapp's business expanded rapidly, but his engines delivered poor performance and were unreliable. The German War Ministry rejected them. The Imperial Austro-Hungarian Army Administration, however, assigned Rapp to manufacture the Austro-Daimler V12 engine under license and appointed Franz Josef Popp to oversee quality control on behalf of the Austrian War Ministry.

Popp soon became involved in running the company, and after Rapp resigned due to ill health in October 1917, he was appointed managing director and the company was reorganized as Bayerische Motoren Werke GmbH (BMW). Popp quickly employed a young Daimler engineer—Max Friz—to design a powerful, high-altitude aero engine. Friz's innovative "overcompressed" 185-horsepower overhead cam, inline six-cylinder BMW IIIa engine featured an altitude-adjusting carburetor that produced a dramatic increase in climb rate and speed at high altitude. It was soon winning dogfights for the Fokker D.VII (Germany's finest World War I fighter plane), earning BMW a reputation for quality it has maintained to the present day.

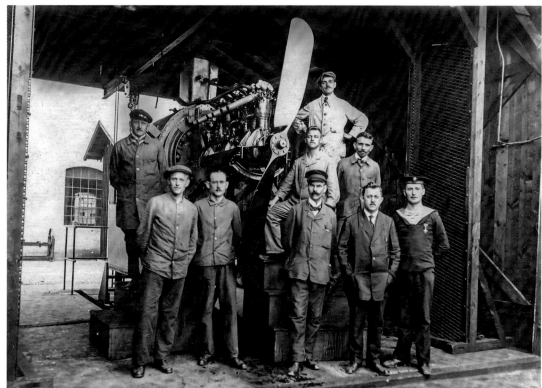

Above Workers, including Austrian sailors, assemble Rapp (left) and Austro-Daimler (right) aircraft engines at the Rapp Motorenwerke, in Munich.

Below Karl Rapp (top right) poses with workers beside a test-bed for the Rapp III aeroengine at Rapp Motorenwerke, Munich, in 1914.

On June 17, 1919, Franz Zeno Diemer set a world record for the highest altitude flown, attaining 9,760 meters (32,020 feet) in a specially developed DFW F 37/III aircraft powered by a 230hp BMW IV radial aero engine. Two weeks later, the Treaty of Versailles prohibited Germany from developing and manufacturing aircraft engines, severely limiting BMW's future. To survive, BMW turned to manufacturing such mundane items as agricultural equipment, truck and boat engines, and braking assemblies for railway cars. Nonetheless, BMW was barely solvent; its employees fell from a wartime high of 3,500 to only a skeleton crew.

End view, with propeller hub (bottom), of the water-cooled BMW IIIa in-line six-cylinder SOHC aircraft engine designed by Max Friz. The 185-horsepower, high-compression motor with innovative altitude-adjusting carburetor gave an astoundingly good climb rate and high-altitude performance, as well as low fuel consumption.

Shop foreman Martin Stolle was a keen motorcyclist who owned a 1914 British Douglas 500cc motorcycle with opposed flat-twin cylinders positioned fore and aft. This intrigued BMW's chief engineer Max Friz, who reverse-engineered the Douglas engine to produce a

portable industrial engine, designated the M2B15, in 1920. With a perfectly square bore and stroke of 68mm, the 494cc M2B15 developed 6.5 horsepower. BMW was soon producing the side-valve boxer twin "Bayern engine" for a number of start-up German motorcycle manufacturers. This included manufacturing Nuremberg-based Victoria-Werke's KR-I. Nonetheless, Popp was keen to refocus his business. Financed by Viennese banker Camillo Castiglioni, in the summer of 1922 he established a newly independent company—BMW AG—with Castiglioni as the major shareholder. The company moved into one of Castiglioni's factories: that of Gustav Otto's still functioning yet struggling Bayerische Flugzeugwerke, which was soon merged with BMW. The current BMW was born. (BFW became a separate company again in 1926 and went on to become Messerschmitt AG in 1938.)

Having likewise been forced to abandon work on aircraft, Otto's BFW had developed a motorized bicycle—the "Flink"—powered by a 148cc two-stroke engine. In 1922, it also began producing the larger Helios motorcycle using BMW's M2B15 motor, about the time the BFW brand was transferred to BMW's ownership. This put BMW in the motorcycle business completely. However, the Helios weak chassis was seriously flawed. BMW was keen to come up with a whole new design.

Opposite *BMW foreman Martin Stolle on a Victoria-Werke KR I powered by a BMW 492cc, 6.5hp, side-valve boxer-twin M2BI5 engine, in 1923.*

Above *A Helios motorcycle made by Gustav Otto's Bayerische Flugzeugwerke (BFW)—later to evolve into Messerschmitt AG—with a BMW M2BI5 engine, in 1926.*

THE BIRTH OF THE BMW BOXER

The "boxer" layout dates back to German engineer Karl Benz's 1897 design for a horizontally opposed, twin-cylinder four-stroke engine in which the two pistons move in opposite directions and reach the top and bottom of their respective

cylinders at the same time (like a boxer pumping his fists) to turn a single crankshaft. Max Friz's M2B15 fore-and-aft boxer copied from the British Douglas design became a template for the first genuine BMW motorcycle and powerplant, and was the first to bear BMW's corporate blue-and-white "propeller" insignia.

Recognizing that the fore-and-aft boxer configuration led the rear cylinder to overheat (and inspired by the 1918 Granville Bradshaw–designed A.B.C. Motors motorcycle with a 400cc flat-twin transverse boxer engine), Friz turned the motor 90 degrees across the frame, putting the cylinders directly in the airstream to improve cooling. The new layout's longitudinal crankshaft made adoption of shaft drive the logical choice, providing a far superior method of delivering driving torque to the rear wheel. Evolved from the M2B15, Friz's new fully encased, 8.5 horsepower, 494cc, side-valve M2B33 boxer engine was placed inside a Friz-designed triangular frame featuring a rigid duplex spine running from steering head to rear hub, with sturdy double-cradle spars running beneath the engine to rejoin the steering head.

BMW's first motorcycle—the R32—was unveiled to acclaim at the Paris Motorcycle Salon in 1923. The elegant and technically advanced R32 was a revelation. None of its features was unique to the R32, which went into production in 1924. But it established the classic transverse boxer foundation of every motorcycle BMW would produce for the next 60 years, and it was unique in Friz's incorporation of so much advanced features. It wasn't especially powerful; top speed was about 95 km/h (58 mph). But the low center of gravity delivered deft handling. The engine's smooth power delivery allowed the R32 to be ridden for extended periods at a time when most motorcycles shook violently enough to crack engine castings and frames. And although it was relatively expensive compared to the competition, no other motorcycle was so superbly engineered. It quickly gained a reputation for outstanding reliability and ease of maintenance. Of course, BMW steadily improved the R32. The company had sold 3,090 models by the time the R32 was replaced in 1926, securing the future of the BMW company.

Above The BMW R32's air-cooled M2B33 opposed-twin boxer engine had cylinders perpendicular to the direction of travel. Its unit construction (with the gearbox connected directly to the engine crankcase) allowed for use of a Cardan shaft drive.

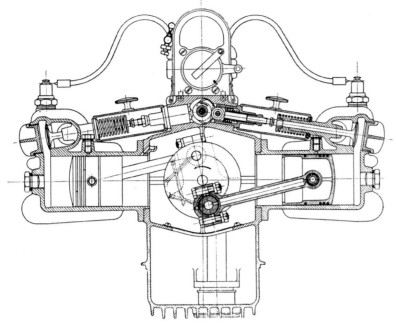

Schnitt durch den Motor

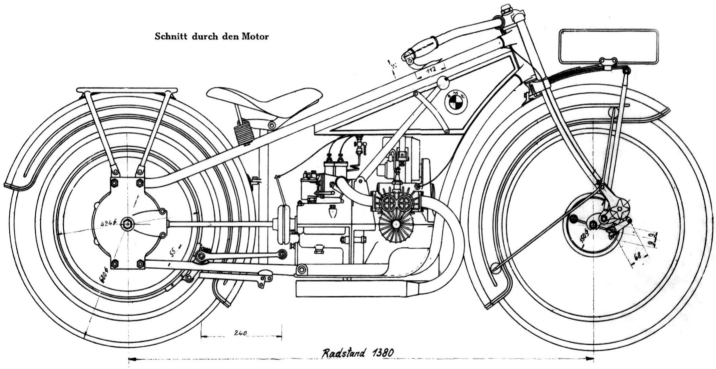

• Model Nomenclature

Before the introduction of the four-cylinder K series bikes in 1983, all BMW motorcycle models were prefixed by the letter R, for "Rad" ("bike")—a German slang derivative of motorrad ("motorcycle"). While the early bikes had no numbering convention, by the 1930s, the nomenclature of the R twin-cylinder boxers evolved to follow logical principles, with the R prefix followed by a numeric code related to engine size. Thus, the 400cc R4 of 1932 preceded the 300cc R3 of 1936, while the R5 (1936) and R6 (1937) were 500cc and 600cc, respectively.

As BMW's model lineup expanded and more specialized boxers were introduced, mode-specific suffixes were added: S for "sporting" models (beginning with the R50S in 1960); T for "touring" (launched with the 1978 R100T); G/S for "dual sport" (Geländestrases, with the 1980 R80G/S); RS (Reisesport) and RT (Reisetourer) for fully faired sportsters and tourers; and even LS (for "luxury sport"). Recent years have seen further expansion of mode-specific suffixes.

Similar conventions and suffixes are applied to the K series and subsequent F series (introduced in the mid-1990s). Newer prefixes include G, for entry-level, single-cylinder models introduced in 2015; S, for inline-four sports bikes; M, for high-performance variants of the S models; and C, for "city" bikes, including CS ("city and street") and CT ("city and tourer") models.

Above *Franz Bieber after winning the 1924 Eifel Race on a BMW R37—a more powerful, higher-compression version of the R32, with a top speed of 118 km/h (73 mph).*

Opposite *BMW's Franz Bieber, Rudi Reich, and Rudolf Schleicher celebrate winning all three classes at the 1924 Solitude Race on their R37s.*

RACING AHEAD

To develop and test its motorcycle technology (and generate headline news to build brand awareness), BMW quickly focused on racing its bikes. When Max Friz and Martin Stolle left

BMW in 1922, motorcycle development was left to young engineer Rudolf Schleicher, a competitive racer. The R32 was no match for Victoria-Werke's KR-2, which trounced BMW in the Stuttgart circuit in 1923. Thus, Schleicher developed a high-performance version of the R32—the R37—using a refined, overhead-valve boxer engine (the M2B36) using aluminum cylinder heads. A three-slide carburetor and an increase in compression to 6.2:1 doubled power to 16 horsepower, giving a top speed of around 118 km/h (70 mph).

The R37 immediately claimed racing victories, with Franz Bieber winning the German Championship in 1924. When Schleicher took the gold medal in the 1926 International Six Day Trials (considered the world's toughest motorcycle sport event), BMW's reputation for competitive success was secured. The R37 was expensive and only 152 were sold. But it established BMW's formula of offering more higher-horsepower sporting overhead-valve variants alongside its more utilitarian and torquey side-valve tourers, using a common chassis.

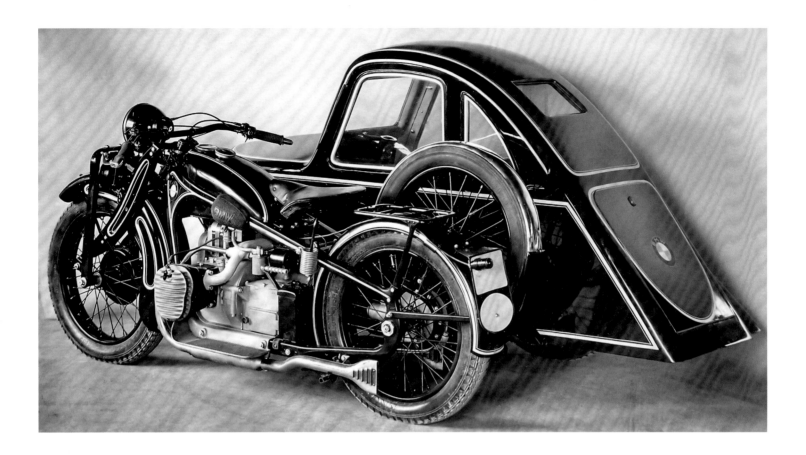

The company felt confident in expanding its model range, beginning in 1925 with the more economical R39, BMW's first single. Engineers simply lopped a cylinder off the R37 overhead-valve twin. Otherwise, the 6.5 horsepower single measured the same 68mm x 68mm bore and stroke and featured the same unit construction engine and transmission, with longitudinal crankshaft and shaft drive. It sold poorly and was discontinued in 1927.

The following year brought the R62 tourer and the R63 sports model, BMW's first 750cc motorcycles. Producing 18 horsepower, the reliable fourth generation heir to the R32 made the R62 the outstanding touring motorcycle of the 1920s, while racing rider Ernst Henne rode a R63 to multiple victories on the track. In 1929, the models were replaced by the R11 tourer and R16 sportster (still powered by upgraded 750cc boxer engines) in a completely new pressed steel frame. BMW's tubular frames used up to that point had suffered from weak joints that were brazed, not welded. The stronger yet heavier, torsion-resistant pressed-steel "star frame" chassis defined BMW's 1930s generation of motorcycles.

BMW resurrected its single-cylinder motorcycles in 1931 with the shaft-driven 198cc R2, which capitalized on a new law intended to revive the depression-era German economy; no license or vehicle tax was required for bikes below 200cc. It featured exposed valve gear and the new, thinner gauge pressed-steel frame. But the R2 was also the first BMW bike to feature an air filter, plus the tunnel-style one-piece crankcase that would become a fixture of BMW air-cooled boxer engines for six decades. A 1932 redesign enclosed the valve springs, and an Amal carburetor boosted power in 1933. Relatively inexpensive yet delivering 95 km/h (59 mph) and 43 km/L (100 mpg), it sold more than 15,000 until discontinued in 1936.

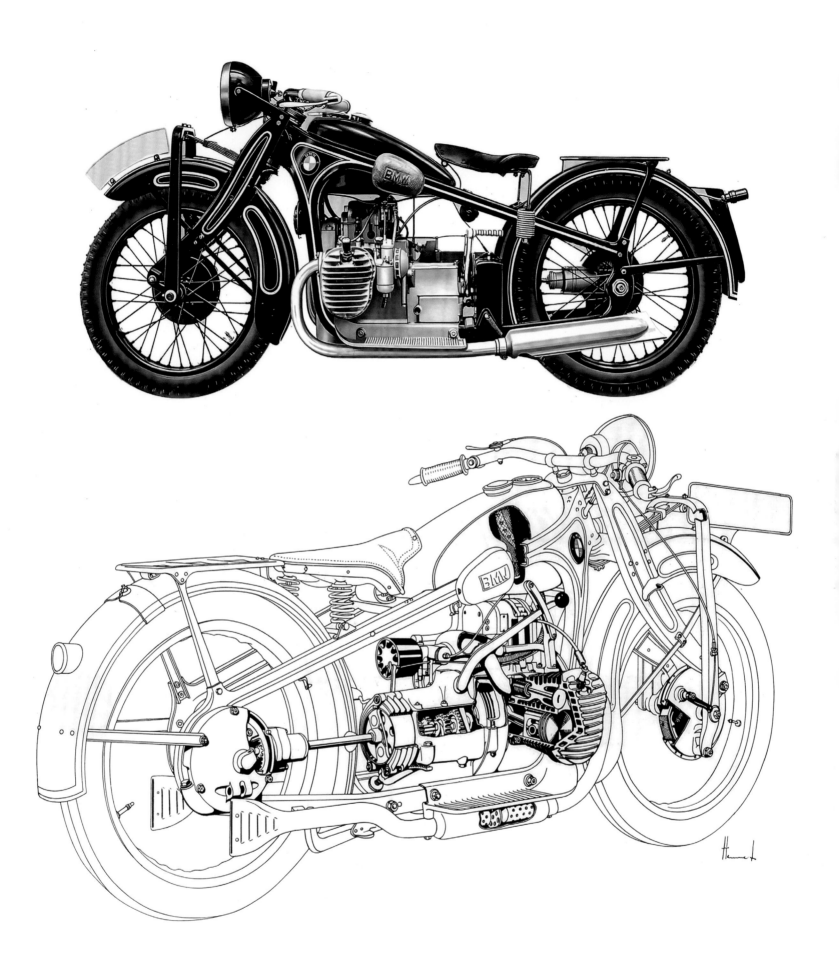

Opposite A 1933 BMW RII tourer with sleek Royal deluxe sidecar.

Above The RII's 745cc side-valve, flathead M56 engine was slung low in a pressed-steel "Star" frame.

Below This 1931 RII's sectional view illustrates how the transverse boxer layout facilitated a Cardan shaft drive.

"My loyal sports comrade – the B.M.W. 750 cc. reads this advertisement in the March 1929 issue of Motor und Sport (Motor and Sport) magazine. Instead of a headlight it features an oversize BMW logo.

Above BMW team rider Ernst Henne splashes through a creek on a R16 during the 1931 German ADAC Three Days Trial.

Below Introduced in 1929, the R16 sportster featured a sprung seat and rigid un-sprung rear frame.

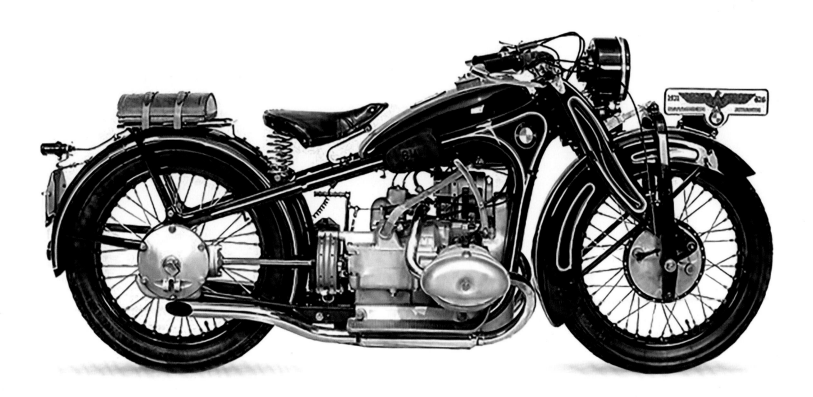

Above Ernst Henne sits proudly atop his 498cc BMW R37 after winning the 1931 International Six Days Reliability Trial, in Germany.

Opposite clockwise from top left On November 28, 1937, Ernst Henne rode a fully faired, supercharged, 495cc R255 Kompressor at 279.5 km/h (173.7 mph) to set a world speed record for motorcycles.

Ernst Henne during a speed-record attempt near Vienna in April 1931.

Ernst Henne and his streamlined R255 Kompressor gets a push-start on the Autobahn near Frankfurt on November 28, 1937.

Ernst Henne poses in white racing gear on his 1937 world-record Kompressor, with cutaway outer fairing.

• Land Speed Records

In 1929, the motorcycle land speed record (207.6 km/h [129 mph]) was held by Herbert Le Vack on an English Brough Superior fitted with a JAP 1,000cc V-twin engine. German champion and BMW team rider Ernst Henne set out to break the record by stripping his R37 and fitting it with BMW's new short-stroke 734cc boxer engine with a Zoller supercharger. Donning a streamlined helmet and tail cone (the bike itself was unfaired), Henne attained a record 216.75 km/h (134.68 mph) on September 19, 1929.

For the next decade, the record see-sawed between various JAP-powered British motorcycles and supercharged Kompressor twins ridden by Henne. Each time his record was broken, Henne and BMW quickly retook the crown. He set 75 records between 1929 and October 21, 1937, when Piero Taruffi throttled his supercharged 492cc Gilera to 274.18 km/h (170.4 mph) for a new world record on Italy's A4 Autostrada. Four weeks later, Henne secured the final pre-war record of 279.51 km/h (173.68 mph) on a 495cc overhead cam R255 Kompressor that produced 108hp at 8,000rpm and had fully faired streamlined bodywork. Henne's record remained unbeaten until 1951.

Adolf Hitler visits the BMW exhibition stand after opening the 1938 Berlin Motor Show.

THE GREAT DEPRESSION AND THE THIRD REICH

By 1929, BMW boasted 3,860 employees and had sold more than 25,000 of the highest-quality motorcycles ever built. In 1926, it has resumed manufacturing aircraft engines, and in 1928, it acquired Automobilwerk Eisenach and introduced its first automobile—the Dixi, a variant of the English Austin 7, built under license. With its diversified product line, BMW survived the Great Depression fairly well, assisted by the rise of Adolf Hitler and his National Socialist Party. The Nazi regime invested huge sums of money in rearming, and BMW's off-road-capable 398cc R4 single (essentially an over-bored R2 with four-speed transmission) was just the kind of rugged and reliable motorcycle the German military needed. Designed specifically for the Wehrmacht, it came with a skid plate and right-side kick stand, but it was affordable and therefore popular with civilians also. Strong sales of the R4 boosted BMW to 11,500 employees by 1935. It was produced (and modified) in five series until replaced in 1936 by the more powerful R12, which was offered with a sidecar.

Radical new models were also being developed. Most notable was the visually stunning R7 (1935), an Art Deco–inspired concept motorcycle sheathed in full monocoque bodywork and fitted with telescopic front forks. Only one R7 was ever made. But telescopic forks with hydraulic shock absorbers made their debut that year with the side-valve R12 replacing the R11, and the sportier overhead-valve R17 replacing the R16. The oil-dampened forks significantly improved ride comfort and allowed the fitting of a smaller 48cm (19in) wheel that made the handling much lighter.

By 1938, BMW had set the industry standard for both road and track. That year, it introduced five new models—a last high-water mark fling before the onset of World War II. A completely new range was launched with the overhead-valve R51, R61, and R66, and the side-valve R71. Each featured a plunger rear-wheel suspension (as used on the Kompressor road racers, see sidebar) and an optional foot-operated gear shift. The flagship model was the R66, powered by a 30hp, overhead-valve, 600cc boxer engine with a single camshaft. With a top speed of 143 km/h (89 mph), it was the fastest BMW motorcycle produced in the prewar period. Nonetheless, it didn't sell well. Buyers preferred the much cheaper R51, or the more reliable R71 (the last BMW powered by a side-valve engine), especially when fitted with a sidecar.

Meanwhile, material shortages were already being felt as prime metals were allocated for war production. Thus, the R66 and siblings sacrificed their chrome-plated parts. A final run of R71s in 1941 brought production of civilian motorcycles to a halt. Thereafter, all the company's motorcycle production was engaged in supplying the Wehrmacht (especially the iconic BMW R75 motorcycle with sidecar rig featuring integral two-wheel drive to both rear wheels). In 1934, production of aero engines had already been transferred to BMW Flugmotorenbau GmbH, which contributed the lion's share of BMW's World War II sales. Its most successful engine (with more than 61,000 built) was the 41.8-liter (2,550ci), 14-cylinder BMW 801 radial engine that powered the Focke-Wulf 190 fighter to 652 km/h (405 mph). BMW was also a pioneer in jet engine design, and its 003 engine powered the Heinkel He 162 Volksjäger, but not the V-1 "flying bomb" for which it was originally intended.

Above *Eduardo Westermayer races a 597cc R66—BMW's fastest pre-war production motorcycle—at high speed in 1939.*

Above An R66 with sidecar races through the Bavarian Alps during the controversial 1939 International Six Day Trials, immediately following Hitler's annexation of Austria.

Below Launched in 1938, the R66 was (along with the R51 and R61) the first BMW production motorcycle to feature a plunger rear-wheel suspension.

28

Opposite This poster celebrates BMW wins in the 1933 and 1934 International Six Day Trials.

Left George Meier on the supercharged BMW RS255 Kompressor, in 1938.

Below left The RS255's supercharger forced pressurized air past valves operated by twin overhead camshafts encased in a compact magnesium cylinder head cover.

Below right The RS255 made extensive use of lightweight magnesium for engine castings.

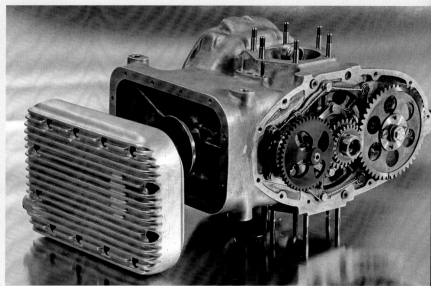

• The RS255 Kompressor

Despite Franz Bieber's and Rudolf Schleicher's victories on their R37s in the early 1920s, English bikes—being nimbler through the corners—dominated the European road race circuit of the time. BMW calculated that an extra burst on the straights could lick the Brits. Starting in 1926, BMW's race bikes began experimenting with Swiss-built Zoller "superchargers" that sat atop the transmission. These small air compressors (driven from the crankshaft) force-fed air into the combustion chamber, hugely increasing fuel-burn efficiency and nearly doubling power output (compression was reduced to 6.0:1 to facilitate high supercharger boost pressure). The blown 500cc boxer produced 55 horsepower; the 750cc motor cranked out a mighty 75 ponies!

The BMW Kompressor motorcycle soon dominated European road racing. By the early 1930s, however, the ever-more nimble and powerful competition was catching up.

The Nazi regime understood the propaganda value of racing and in 1935 sponsored development of a second generation Kompressor: the RS255. Using BMW's basic boxer architecture, the 492cc engine was specifically designed to be supercharged. The supercharger was now driven directly from the end of the crankshaft at the front of the engine. The twin overhead cam engine featured an undersquare 66mm x 72mm bore and stroke and a new foot-shift, four-speed gearbox. The RS255 also used BMW's new hydraulic damped telescopic fork. That year, the BMW team won the gold medal in the International Six Day Trials, held in Oberstdorf, Germany. But the Kompressor won few track races, despite being the fastest motorcycle: handling shortfalls still kept the factory team off the podium.

The addition of plunger rear suspension in 1937 provided far better handling, and BMW's race team began winning Grands Prix. In 1938, George Meier won the German and European Championships. The following year, he took the checkered flag in the Senior TT at the Isle of Man (the first non-Briton to win the world's most prestigious race), with BMW teammate Jock West taking silver.

It was the end of the road for the mighty Kompressors. World War II put an end to motor sports in Europe for half a decade. When motorcycle racing resumed, supercharged engines were banned.

R32

Introduced as "the touring bike from Bayerische Motoren Werke" at the 1923 Paris Salon, BMW's first motorcycle set the template of design, innovation, and engineering excellence that would define the German marque. Although Max Friz had designed the R32 in only five weeks, it was an eye-catching masterpiece that in many ways was years ahead of the competition.

Friz designed the R32 with reliability, durability, and ease of maintenance foremost. Slung within a rigid triangular frame, its signature feature was an air-cooled, side-valve, pushrod-operated, opposed-twin boxer engine with cylinders horizontal to the direction of travel.

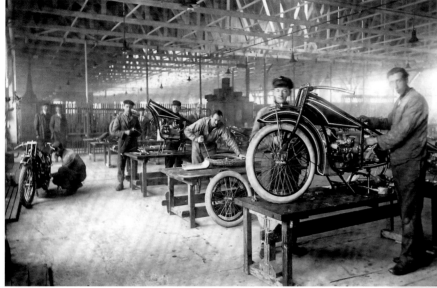

Above Production of the first R32 motorcycles began at BMW's Munich plant in 1924.

Right BMW's rider Rudi Reich on a 1924 test run with an unpainted R32.

This orientation allowed the three-speed gearbox to be bolted direct to the engine crankcase (which housed the flywheel and clutch). This "unit" construction allowed Friz to install a robust Cardan shaft drive in lieu of the traditional primary drive system and chain final drive that almost all motorcycle manufacturers used. This was far less vulnerable to dirt, sand, and mud, and made wheel and tire changes easier. In fact, the entire R32 was easy to work on and rapidly gained a reputation for reliability.

Applying his experience in aero engineering, Friz employed new lightweight alloys in the engine's pistons and cylinder heads. He also adopted a single carburetor with two slides (one for each cylinder) of BMW's own design mounted on top of the engine. And at a time when most manufacturers used total-loss oiling systems requiring riders to add oil at regular intervals, the R32 featured a high-tech wet-sump design that circulated oil to the engine via a geared oil pump.

The 486cc M2B33 boxer had the same perfectly square 68mm x 68mm bore and stroke measurements as the M2B15 powerplant from which it derived. It also retained circular side-valve cylinder heads with deep finning, into which finned plugs were screwed to allow easy access for valve maintenance.

The front inverted leaf-spring suspension atop the front mudguard was similar to that used by America's Indian Motorcycle Company, with forks curving fore of the axles, to which they were connected by short sprung tailing arms. A sprung seat compensated for the lack of rear suspension. The bike's major flaw was its poor (and outdated) braking. It lacked a front brake entirely (in 1925, the series 2 R32 gained a mechanically operated expanding-shoe front brake), while ineffectual rear braking was provided by a wooden wedge-block that pressed against a dummy wheel rim, with direct drive to the shoe from a right-side pedal.

Weighing 120 kg (264 lbs), the R32 was heavy compared to its contemporaries. But it delivered very secure handling, thanks not least to the engine being slung low in the chassis. With a compression ratio of 5.0:1, the M2B23 engine was enlarged to 494cc in 1925 and produced 8.5 horsepower at a lowly 3,300 rpm. The R32 had a top speed of 95 km/h (58 mph) and could cruise all day long at 64 km/h (40 mph) while delivering a respectable 128 km/L (80 mpg) from its 14-liter (3.7 gallons) tank slung beneath the tubular frame—an important consideration in economically challenged post–World War I Germany.

Priced at 2,200 Reichsmarks, the R32 was considerably more expensive than most rivals. But it was an instant success, selling 1,500 in 1924 and more than 3,100 by the time it was replaced with the 12hp R42 in 1926.

R39

BMW's twin-cylinder R32 was one of the most expensive motorcycles on the market when it launched in 1923. The sportier and more exclusive R37 of 1925 was far pricier (2,900 Reichsmarks), and only 152 were sold before production ceased. That summer, the company turned its sights to less well-heeled buyers and introduced the single-cylinder R39, its third model, which made its debut at the Berlin Motor Show.

The 247cc engine was effectively half that of the R37's OHV M2B36 boxer twin, with the motor mounted longitudinally in the frame but with a single cylinder rising vertically, rather than horizontally as with the boxer. It kept the R37 engine's 68mm x 68mm bore and stroke, and 6.0:1 compression, and used the same alloy overhead-valve cylinder heads, but it breathed through a BMW Spezial 20mm carburetor.

Other than the upright cylinder, the R39 shared the same overall architecture and build quality as its twin-cylinder brethren. The frame was essentially the same twin-tube design as the R32, with the same short swing fork for the front wheel, wire-spoked wheels, whitewall tires, and a crude four-leaf spring front suspension. The rear end remained rigid.

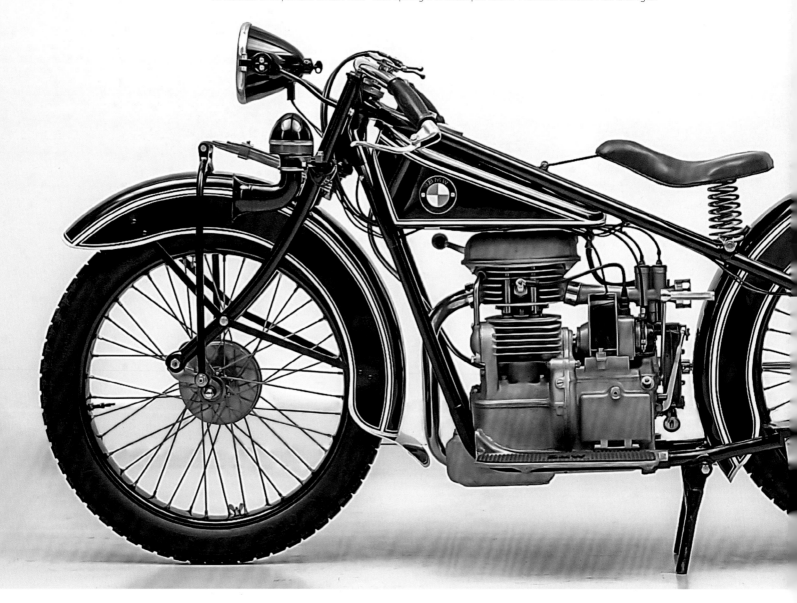

Opposite left BMW's first single was effectively half the R37 twin engine, but with a vertical cylinder, laid in the same frame.
Opposite right Rudi Reich astride a BMW R39 at the 1925 Stuttgart Solituderren (Solitude Race).

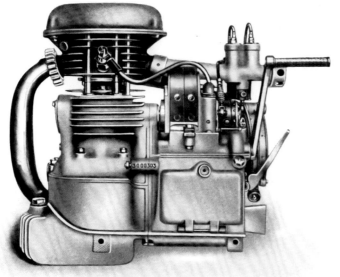

The engine featured a Bosch magneto generator, wet-sump oiling, and shaft drive via a three-speed gearbox bolted directly to the crankcase and driven through a single-disc dry clutch mounted to the flywheel. The braking was a welcome improvement on the boxer twins: the R39 received a mechanical drum brake up front, while the rear brake was now an external Cardan shoe acting on a drum on the driveshaft, rather than the crude wedge-shaped brake block and dummy-rim setup of the R32.

Although priced well below the R32 at 1,870 Reichsmarks, the 250cc R39 offered outstanding performance. Power output was only 6.5 horsepower at 4,000rpm, but tipping the scale at just 110 kg (242 lbs) and with a top speed of around 100 km/h (62 mph), it easily outran the more expensive R32 boxer. The sporty single soon joined the R37 atop racetrack podiums, notably when Josef Stelzer (reputed to be the inventor of the handlebar-installed turning throttle) won the 250cc German Road Championship in 1925 on a racing version of the R39 single.

The R39 consolidated BMW's reputation for exceptional reliability. Nonetheless, while sales were initially strong, excessive oil consumption and cylinder bore wear were problematic, and sales dwindled. Only 855 had been produced by the time construction ended in 1927. It would be four years before BMW introduced another single.

R62/R63

1928

By 1928, BMW was already in the habit of introducing innovative new models on an annual basis. That year, it presented its first 750cc production motorcycles with the side-valve R62 tourer and its stablemate overhead-valve R63 sports model joining the two 500cc models. They were considered the most refined of all the early R series. BMW's reputation for reliability helped ensure that the R62 was soon regarded as *the* outstanding touring motorcycle of the 1920s, while the R63 was the highest performing BMW motorcycle yet.

The bikes were the last generation of BMWs to use the light and strong, all-welded, bent-tube "flat tanker" frames with a triangular gas tank mounted between the engine and top frame. Hence, they were the last models whose sparse yet elegant Bauhaus look provided a clear visual link to the R32 of 1923. In all other regards, they were a huge improvement whose new designs laid the foundation for all big-touring BMWs to come.

The R62's new side-valve 745cc engine closely resembled that of its smaller sibling, the 486cc R52, but with a longer stroke (for a 78mm x 78mm square bore and stroke) and 5.5:1 compression. It generated 18 horsepower at 3400rpm and had much more torque than the R52, with a top speed of 115 km/h (70 mph). The pistons were still cast iron, but BMW's new range-topping R63 Sportmodell used aluminum pistons, and cylinder heads featured a new mounting system.

Above Two BMW R63 sidecar outfits await the start of a race in Bra, Italy, in 1932.

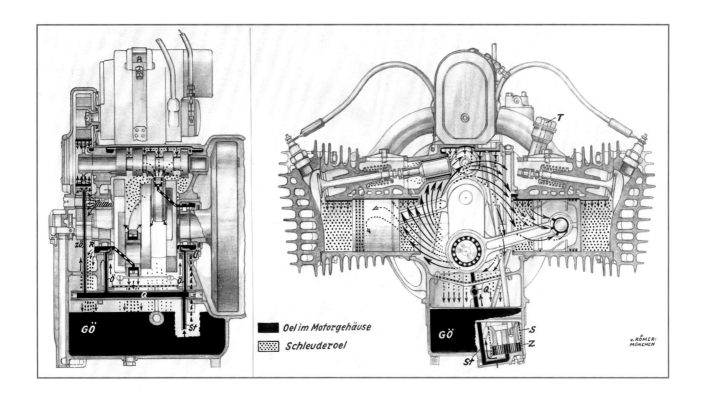

Oel im Motorgehäuse
Schleuderoel

The R63 also retained the R52's short 68mm stroke but with a wider 83mm bore for 734cc, and 6.2:I compression, which gave a top speed of around 120 km/h (75 mph)—making the high-revving OHV model one of the fastest motorcycles available in 1928. Both bikes breathed through a Spezial two-valve 24mm carburetor and had chromed dual fishtail exhausts.

BMW introduced a side-mounted kick-start (kicking out, not down) for the first time. Both bikes also got a redesigned (and stronger) oil lubricated three-speed gearbox, available with optional sidecar final-drive gearing. Shifting was via a right-side hand shifter that BMW would retain until the R5 of 1936. The single-plate clutch was upgraded to a twin plate in 1929.

The entire 1928 lineup—the R52, R57, R62, and R63—had a magneto generator electrical system, with optional Bosch lighting (which became standard for 1929 models). The R62 and R63 also got a larger front brake and a bulkier six-leaf spring for the trailing-link fork. BMW also introduced a hinged door beneath the gearbox that held a toolbox.

BMW's top of the tourer line sold for 1,650 Reichsmarks (approximately the average salary for a German at the time), only about 10 percent more than an R52. It sold well: 4,355 machines had been built by the time the R62 was replaced in 1929 by the RII with pressed-steel frame. Priced at 2,100 Reichsmarks, the R63 also sold well, due partly to its sporting success, including Ernst Henne's giving BMW its first motorcycle speed record of 216.75 km/h (134.68 mph) on a supercharged R63.

Opposite Oil-circuit diagram for the R62 engine.

Right Travelers with an R62 (left) and BMW sidecar unit in Germany (1928).

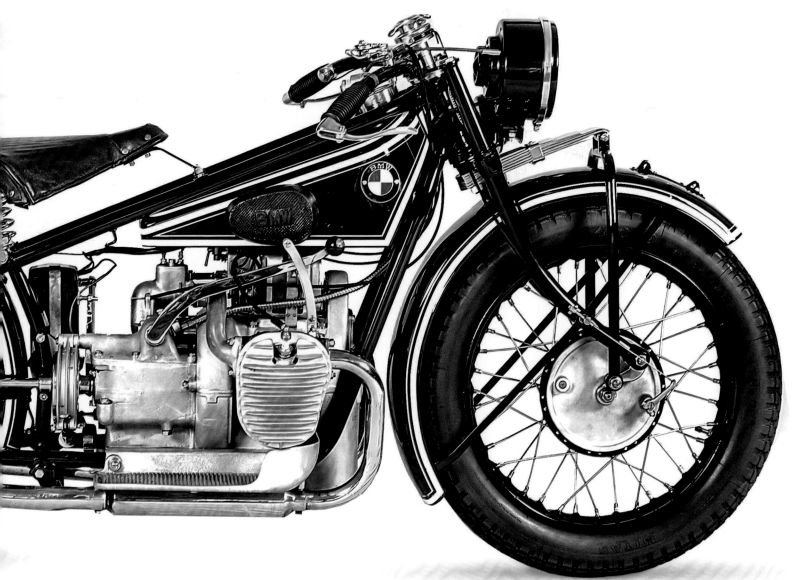

R7

1934

If Batman had been conceived in 1934 instead of in 1939, it's easy to imagine that the almost mythical R7 might have been his first "Batcycle." Styled at the height of Art Deco's Streamline Moderne period, BMW's radical one-off concept bike pushed the aesthetic conventions of motorcycle design to the limit and introduced the world to technology that was far ahead of its time.

Created by BMW's visionary chief design engineer Alfred Böning, it was built to explore futuristic technologies and showcase the bold styling ambition and technical advances that BMW's engineers could achieve. Fueled in part by the propagandist prestige projects of the Nazi era, it was conceived the same year as the Volkswagen Beetle. Many of the R7's features derived from the Bauhaus automotive designs of the era.

Böning's swoopy design proved pressed-steel frames could be uber-stylish. Most dramatic was its aerodynamic monocoque bodywork tapering from the steering head to the rear axle. The transmission, shaft drive, and upper motor were entirely enclosed in expansive aluminum-alloy panes that seemed to merge into the valanced rear mudguard. A gleaming chrome gas tank cover peeked above the R7's curving form (the tank was hidden within the expansive bodywork, as were all the electric components), echoed by twin streamlined "faired-in" fishtail chrome exhausts. Even the taillight was carefully sculpted, exalting a dynamic new world on the move.

The R7's engineering was as eye-popping as its styling. Beneath the swoopy enclosed bodywork lurked an all-new "800" (793cc) OHV, four-valve boxer twin—the M205/I. Designed by engineer Leonhard Ischinger, the oversquare 83mm x 78mm (3.27in × 2.87in) engine featured a tunnel crankcase (a first for BMW) with a forged, one-piece crankshaft. As in car engines, the con-rod big ends were split and ran on plain bearings.

R7

And, uniquely for BMW, the cylinders and heads were one piece (per aero-engine practice at the time), eliminating the need for head gaskets. The camshafts were now located below the crank, which placed the push-rod tubes below the cylinders, permitting the cylinders to be positioned for higher ground clearance in corners while providing a preferential placement of the valves and spark plugs. The experimental model gave seriously hot performance, delivering an impressive 35 horsepower at 5,000rpm and a top speed of 145 km/h (90 mph).

Even the controls and chromed instruments were radically new. The headlight housed an elliptical rotating disc digital speedometer inspired by prestige automobiles of the era. The top cover sported a chromed fuel filler cap and oil pressure gauge. On the right-hand side rose a car-style gear-shift lever—another radical first for BMW—in the already-standard automotive H pattern. The R7 boasted a four-speed transmission and a dry, single plate, cable-operated clutch.

The R7 was also the first motorcycle in the world to be fitted with hydraulically damped telescopic front forks (soon to become standard on all BMW's boxers). But there was still no rear suspension; the rider was cushioned by a sprung saddle.

Although a single prototype was built, the futuristic concept bike with a sexy curvaceous appeal never went into production. It was dismantled then lost during World War II until rediscovered in 2005, when it was painstakingly restored by BMW. It now takes pride of place in the BMW Museum, in Munich. Nonetheless, many of the R7's novel features soon appeared on production models, beginning with the R5.

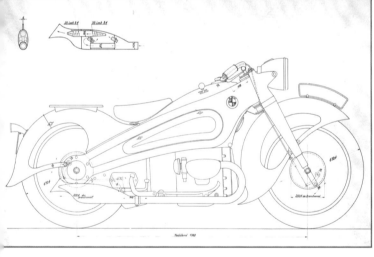

Below The R7 prototype introduced the motorcycling world's first-ever telescopic fork, while the striking body featured an extensive Art Deco shell atop a pressed-steel frame.

R12/R17

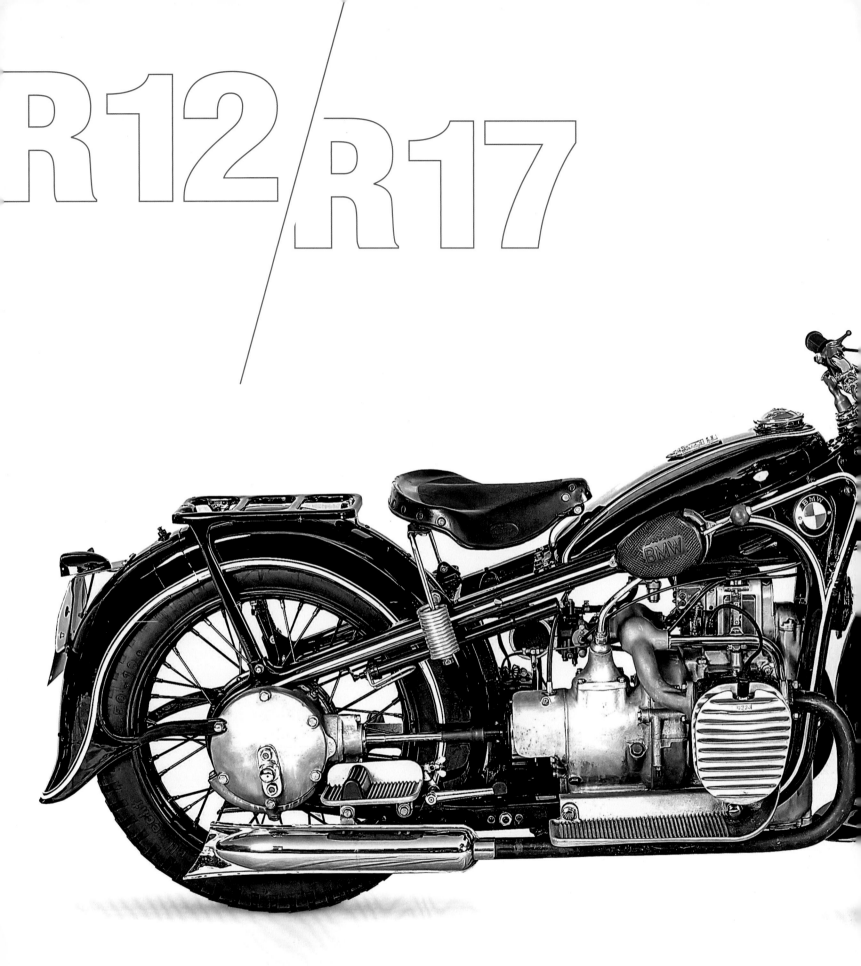

Above Oil-dampened telescopic forks debuted in 1935 with the side-valve R12 and sportier overhead-valve R17.
Opposite The 745cc, side-valve R12 with sidecar was rugged and reliable. The single-carb Einvergasermotor version supplied the German Wehrmacht until supplanted by the R75.

Introduced at the 1935 Berlin Motor Show (the fourth such show held under the Nazi regime was opened in ceremonial style by Adolf Hitler), the 745cc R12 and its sportier and more expensive R17 sibling were developed from the preceding R11 and R16 series of 1931. The newer models retained the robust, Art Deco–style pressed-steel frame chassis, but also introduced new chassis and drivetrain technology.

Most notably, the R12 and R17 were motorcycle milestones as the world's first production bikes to feature oil-dampened telescopic front forks. BMW's pioneering forks had evolved for racing in 1934 and were then patented before being introduced to the mass market (after World War II, the patents essentially became spoils of war for the Allies). The fork significantly improved rideability and comfort compared to the former flat spring rocker. Nonetheless, despite this state-of-the-art front-end design, the old R11's and R16's rigid un-sprung rear setup was retained (rear shock absorbers and springs wouldn't appear until 1938).

The R12 replaced the R11 as BMW's touring motorcycle. It was powered by the same basic 745cc side-valve, flathead M56 engine, but now came in two options: either a single, SUM-carbed 18hp version capable of 110 km/h (67 mph), or a dual Amal-carb version producing 22hp and attaining 120 km/h (75 mph). The single-carb R12s used a magneto ignition that functioned independently of the battery; the twin-carb version used a battery and coil ignition.

The R17, with its 736cc OHV engine, generated 33 horsepower and had a top speed of 140 km/h (86 mph)—one of the fastest production bikes of its time.

The engines were wed to a new four-speed transmission, operated by a hand-shift lever on the fuel tank's right side. By 1935, this was outdated. Although American large displacement V-twins still used hand-operated shifters, most European motorcycle manufacturers had already switched to foot-shift transmissions. The R12 and R17, however, were fitted with a new rear drum-brake system (gone was the ineffective Cardan brake, which applied braking force to the driveshaft). The rear drum and wheel were the same size as the front, so the 48cm (19in) wheels were now interchange-able and could also use the same tires.

The R12 was primarily a civilian machine. In 1937, however, the single-carb Einvergasermotor version was adopted by the Wehrmacht (many were equipped with a sidecar on the right side) and remained in production up to 1942, when it was superseded by the R75. In all, 36,008 R12s were built, making it the most widely sold pre-war BMW motorcycle. In comparison, the R17 was expensive and only 434 were built before production ceased in 1937.

Opposite The 736cc OHV R17 was powerful and fast, but it didn't sell well; only a few hundred were made.

Above German rider W. Reinhardt steers an R17 with sidecar in the 1937 International Six Days Trial, in Wales.

R5

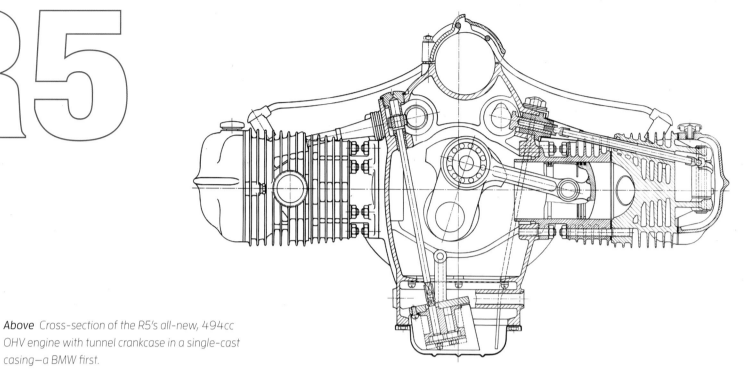

Above Cross-section of the R5's all-new, 494cc OHV engine with tunnel crankcase in a single-cast casing—a BMW first.

By 1936, BMW was already heavily invested in military motorcycle production. But one look at the R5 reveals that the company's engineers were capable of producing one of the most advanced bikes of the decade while also serving the "keep-it-simple" needs of the Wehrmacht. The innovative R5 was BMW's first new 500cc sports model in six years, and despite its short life, it was a sensation and destined to be one of the great bikes of its decade. Its creator, BMW engineer Rudolf Schleicher, considered it his most important design.

For one, its forward-leaning styling seemed two decades ahead of its time. Its sophisticated "1950s" look was defined by a new elliptical twin-cradle frame of arc-welded oval-shaped tubes. Adapted directly from BMW's racing machines, it offered exceptional torsional stiffness. It was also much lighter than the pressed-steel frames of earlier models: the R5 tipped the scales at a modest 165 kg (363 lbs).

The R5's cutting-edge features included the state-of-the-art telescopic forks with hydraulic damping adjustment first seen on Alfred Böning's sensational R7 concept bike. Front-wheel travel was limited. And rear suspension was still limited to the sprung saddle from the R7 concept bike (in 1938, the plunger rear suspension developed on the race machines was finally added to the R5—and the bike was renamed the R51). But the new front suspension greatly improved wheel control, roadholding, and the bike's overall nimble and sporty handling. It was a charm to ride.

The R5 received a complex new race-proven version of the familiar 494cc OHV boxer-twin powerplant cased, for the first time, in a single-cast housing. The all-new engine with advanced tunnel crankcase kept the traditional square 68mm bore x 68mm stroke and retained overhead valves, now actuated by twin chain-driven camshafts. This allowed for more advantageous valve angles and shorter pushrods, which combined with new hairpin valve-springs from BMW's race bikes to produce higher revs. New cylinder head assemblies included rocker arm bearings cast into the heads. The cylinders each breathed through its own Amal S/423 carburetor. With a compression ratio of 6.7:1, power output was an impressive 24hp at 5,500rpm, and its top speed of 135 km/h (84 mph) rivaled that of BMW's 750cc models.

England's Velocette had first introduced a positive-stop foot-operated gearshift in 1928. With the R5, it made its BMW debut as a left-side shift lever for the four-speed transmission. (It also featured an archaic hand-shift lever sprouting on the right side of the transmission case, which unfathomably survived through 1955.)

By far BMW's most advanced motorcycle to date, priced at 1,550 Reichsmarks it cost less than the R57, the company's last 500cc sports model, which ended production in 1929. Despite representing excellent value, only 2,652 had been sold when production ceased in 1937 to make way for the R51, with its new rear suspension.

R35

Although BMW pre–World War II development focused on its large-displacement boxer twins, the company also introduced several shaft-driven singles as entry level models and for riders wanting economical transportation. The 247cc R39 of 1925 was followed by the 200cc R2 (1931–1936), the 398cc R4 (1932–1937), the 305cc R3 (1936), and the 192cc R20 (1937–1938). All were closely related to their boxer cousins and shared their chassis, engine, suspension, and other components.

The R4 had closed the gap between small and large models, and being both reliable and bulletproof had proved popular with the German military, helping BMW weather the depression. The 342cc R35 was introduced in 1937 to replace the R4, upon which it was closely based. Although it featured some refinements, such as telescopic forks, BMW's latest single was designed to appeal to both civilians and the conservative Wehrmacht. At its core was a vertical-cylinder OHV R4 engine with a 4mm (0.157in) reduction in bore to 72mm (2.834in) and a displacement of 342cc. A small power increase over the old, proven R4 delivered 14 horsepower at 4,500rpm, a similar top speed of 100 km/h (61 mph), and—weighing just 155 kg (341 lbs)—an economical 33 km/L (78 mpg).

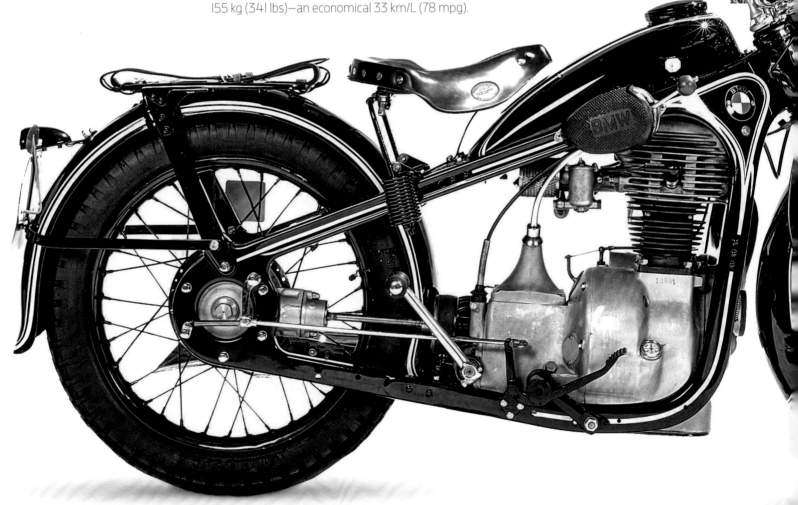

Opposite Most R35s were sold to the Wehrmacht and to police forces as far afield as the South Seas (seen here).

1937

The engine was wed to a four-speed transmission controlled via a shift-lever on the right side. It also had a right-side kick-start.

Even though the R5 and R6 boxers (and even the budget R20 single) had already launched with lightweight twin-loop tubular frames, the R35 was the last BMW model to use a heavy and sturdy pressed steel frame. It *did* get telescopic forks (a vast improvement over the R4's basic cantilever leaf-spring forks). But since the R35 was a budget model, the forks had no hydraulic damping. The only rear suspension was still the sprung seat.

Although the R35 was already outdated, as a sober and solid performer it sold well. The Wehrmacht bought the bulk of the 15,000 R35s produced between 1937 and 1940 (primarily as dispatch bikes), when BMW's entire motorcycle effort was focused on producing the military R75. After World War II, BMW's Eisenach assembly plant was taken over by the Soviets, who continued to produce the R35—labeled as "BMW"—as a spoil of war using existing stock. BMW sued in 1952 after being granted permission by the Allies to resume production. The East Germans simply rebranded as Eisenacher Motorenwerk, changed the BMW logo from blue to red, and continued production under the EMW marque. That year, a foot-operated gear change was adopted, followed in 1953 by a plunger rear suspension. More than 80,000 had been built by the time production ceased in 1955.

R23

As World War II loomed on the horizon, BMW released its last pre-war single—the R23—in 1938. It was the third iteration of a class of motorcycles, beginning with the 198cc R2 in 1931, that took advantage of a German exemption (starting in 1928) from motor vehicle tax for motorcycles up to 200cc and that required no motorcycle license for their riders. Priced at just 975 Reichsmarks, the high-quality R2 with pressed steel frame sold more than 15,000 units. In 1937, the R20 replaced the best-selling R2. It was BMW's first bike to have a bolted tubular frame, the R20's redesigned OHV engine kicked out 8 horsepower, and it had a top speed of 95 km/h (58 mph).

Above *An unidentified rider with his R23 in Africa.*

1938

However, the R20 lasted only one year. In June 1938, the exemption was removed, and a new motorcycle license class was created for motorcycles up to 250cc. BMW therefore developed the R23 to fill this niche. The chassis and motor were based on the R20, whose 60mm x 68mm engine was bored to hold an 8mm bigger piston, bringing the capacity to 247cc (15.lci). The four-stroke, pushrod-operated, two-valve engine with 6.75:1 compression produced 10 horsepower at 5,400rpm and gave a top speed of 95 km/h (58 mph)—the same as the R20.

In almost every other regard, the R23 was identical to the R20. It had battery ignition and a left-side kick-start, and breathed through an 18.2mm Amal carburetor. It came with a three-speed gearbox with a foot gearshift and BMW's trademark Cardan shaft drive (the first chain-driven BMW didn't appear until the 1994 introduction of the F650). It also inherited the R20's undamped R35-type telescopic front fork, with sprung seat for rear suspension. As it was a near identical twin to the R20, BMW even offered a conversion kit for owners to convert their R20s to 247cc.

However, the R23 had a cleaner and tidier look than the R20 as the ungainly toolbox atop the latter's fuel tank was now recessed inside the R23's 9.6-liter (2.5 gallons) tank.

By BMW standards, it seemed bargain-priced at 750 Reichsmarks, and an impressive 8,021 were sold before the outbreak of World War II meant its demise in 1940. When World War II ended, it formed the blueprint for design of the R24—BMW's first motorcycle after production recommenced in 1948.

1940

1968

THE WAR YEARS AND TROUBLED REBIRTH

MILITARY MOTORCYCLES

Production of civilian motorcycles in Germany ground to a halt in 1940 as the country's economy was redirected to meet the needs of the German armed forces. As the Wehrmacht stormed across western Europe in 1940, its principal BMW motorcycle was the side-valve 745cc R12 sidecar hauler. Production of the outdated R12 ended in 1942 after the first BMW R75 sidecar combinations began to roll off the Munich assembly line in 1941.

The R75 had been in development since 1938, when both BMW and Zündapp of Nuremberg were commissioned to design a more effective 750cc sidecar military motorcycle. The requirements were very specific. First, the bike had to be powerful enough to carry three soldiers and their gear, corresponding to a load of 500 kg (1,100 lbs). It had to be robust enough to negotiate rough off-road terrain, to operate for long periods at slow marching speeds without overheating, and, if necessary, to do so while using inferior fuel. Inevitably, the bike had to be uber-reliable.

While Zündapp developed its KS750 boxer twin, BMW engineers worked on creating the R75, intended to be powered by a version of the R71's 750cc side-valve engine. In February 1941, BMW finished developing its prototype, but with an entirely new OHV 750cc engine (after World War II, it would be the basis for the R51/3, R67, and R68 boxers), and the first production bikes left the Munich factory that July. Shortly thereafter, motorcycle production was moved to BMW's Eisenach plant, as the larger Munich facility was needed for aircraft engine production.

Although the R75 could function in appalling conditions and was extremely dependable, the Wehrmacht selected the Zündapp KS750 as the better machine. It instructed BMW to cease making the expensive-to-produce R75 and to build the KS750 (with its strong parallelogram fork) under license. Although the R75's telescopic front forks were too weak for the heavy loads, BMW's large in-house stock of forks earned the R75 a reprieve. Nevertheless, the BMW and Zündapp machines shared two-thirds of their parts in common due to the Wehrmacht's mandatory standardization requirement.

Production continued at Eisenach using Nazi slave laborers. As a consequence, production numbers and quality suffered. In 1943, the Wehrmacht placed its final order for 2,000 machines at 2,000 Reichsmarks apiece. BMW was to cease R75 production by May 1944. This was later amended to the close of 1944 as Allied bombing began to interrupt production. After three raids that summer, the Eisenach factory was so badly damaged that production of the R75 ended on October 18, 1944. In all, approximately 18,000 R75s had been built for the German military.

BMW's Munich facility at Milbertshofen, which had been making aero engines, was also destroyed. The company, therefore, was in a desperate situation after the war, when it came under Allied jurisdiction as part of the American occupation zone. The Eisenach facility was located in the Soviet zone, which would soon become East Germany. The Soviets took possession as a spoil of war and in 1946 produced some R75s for their own use from salvaged parts. They also produced the M72 military sidecar motorcycle based on BMW's plans for the R71, which had been shared with the Soviets following the 1949 Molotov-Ribbentrop Pact.

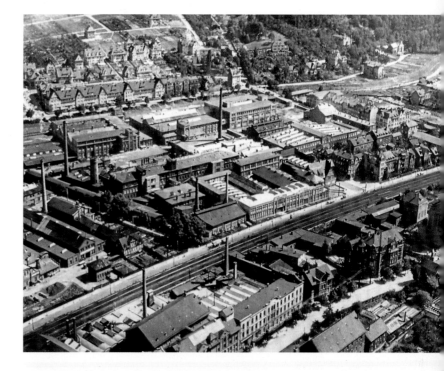

Opposite A 1943 Motor und Sport *magazine cover shows Wehrmacht soldiers crossing a river on an R75.*

Above *Aerial view of BMW's Eisenach assembly plant before World War II.*

Below *BMW's damaged Eisenach factory in 1945 following Allied air raids.*

BMW REBORN

In 1947, when the American occupying forces permitted BMW to resume production of 250cc motorcycles, the company began by building a small number of pre-war R23 singles from a stock of spare parts. However, most of the BMW motorcycle blueprints had been destroyed by Allied bombing raids or lost to the Soviets when they took over the Eisenach factory. BMW therefore reverse-engineered a pre-war R23 to prepare new blueprints. It then used these to design the company's first new post-war motorcycle, the 247cc R24 single.

Due to a shortage of materials, the R24 prototype revealed at the Geneva Motor Show in March 1948 featured many well-disguised wooden components. Germans with money to spare needed affordable transportation, and small displacement motorcycles were in high demand. BMW's pre-war reputation for quality and racing success remained intact, and the response to the R24's release was so great that BMW took 2,500 advance orders. After much delay, it finally began

rolling off the restored Munich assembly lines in December 1948. The following year, more than 9,400 R24s were sold, aided by BMW factory rider George "Schorsch" Meier's racing success in the German Championships on a pre-war RS255 Kompressor.

As new machine tools were acquired to replace those lost by bombing and reparation seizures, BMW's 800-strong workforce was soon building 50 R24s per week. R24 production ended in May 1950, when it was replaced by the more refined R25—the first BMW single to feature plunger rear-wheel suspension inherited from the pre-war boxer twins. Post-war pent-up demand was so great that more than 23,000 were sold in its first year alone. In all, more than 45,000 were built during the series's six-year lifetime, ending with the last R25/3 in 1955.

Meanwhile, in 1950, the American occupying forces ended restrictions on BMW's production of larger displacement motorcycles. The company immediately updated the pre-war 494cc R51 and relaunched it as the R51/2 using the predecessor's chassis and a totally redesigned, single-cam, twin-carb OHV engine. More than 5,000 R51/2s sold that year. The following year, BMW unveiled the R51/3 Sportmodell at the Amsterdam Motor Show. The company also decided to compete in the International Six Days Trial, in Varese, Italy, for the first time since 1939. Team rider Walter Zeller won the silver medal on a tuned model with high-rise exhaust (supercharging was no longer allowed), reaffirming BMW's credentials for handling, reliability, and endurance.

Also new for 1951, the sedate R67—BMW's first post-war 600cc model—was intended as a budget sidecar motorcycle. Underpowered, it was superseded in 1952 by the more robust R67/2. BMW's show-stealer at the Frankfurt Motor Show in October 1951 was the long-awaited and enthralling new sportster R68, which could finally compete with the powerful British 650cc twins, being BMW's first production bike with a top speed exceeding 160 km/h (100 mph). It sold well, notwithstanding its 4,000 Deutsche Mark price tag.

BMW R 25 TOUREN 250ccm ALLRADGEFEDERT

BMW R 51/2 TOUREN-SPORT 500ccm ALLRADGEFEDERT

MOTORRÄDER AUS MÜNCHEN

SCHLENZIG

Opposite R25s began rolling off BMW's Munich assembly line in May 1950.

Right In 1950, BMW produced just two models: the 250cc R25 tourer and 500cc R51/2 sports tourers.

• Racing and Speed Records

BMW was out of the running in the land-speed records of the 1950s and '60s, which were dominated by the NSU Delphin supercharged "Streamliners" and bullet-shaped Triumphs. It also struggled to take the post-war checkered flag on the international Grand Prix circuit, as Germany was initially forbidden from international competition, and when readmitted to the Fédération Internationale de Motocyclisme (IMF) in 1951, supercharging was banned.

BMW also needed a new engine and chassis if it was to be competitive. In 1951, it introduced the new Rennsport RS54 racer, powered by a 50-horsepower, long-stroke Type 253 engine with double overhead cams and oversize carburetors. It met great success as a sidecar rig, winning 18 world championships in the next two decades, helmed by Max Klankermeier and Ludwig Kraus. But as a solo machine, it couldn't match the Hondas and MV Agustas that dominated GP world championships in the five IMF displacement classes (50cc, 125cc, 250cc, 350cc, and 500cc) ridden by Mike Hailwood and Giacomo Agostini—among the greatest competition riders of all time.

In 1953, the Earles fork suspension was adopted for the 253cc with fuel injection, magnesium crankcases, and redesigned cylinder heads. The short-stroke 253f (1956–1960) with 11:1 Mahle pistons pumped out 60 horsepower at 9,000rpm. In 1956, Walter Zeller rode it to second place in the 500cc World Championship despite the Earles-type fork's idiosyncratic handling, while Wilhelm Noll and Fritz Cron raced their sidecar version to their second world championship title. The following year, Fritz Hillebrand and Manfred Grünwald repeated BMW's sidecar championship success, and John Lewis and Bruce Daniels beat the highly favored British 650-twins to win the prestigious Thruxton 500 on a production R69 model with sidecar. BMW engineers' attention was increasingly diverted to sidecar racing, and in 1958, the company withdrew from two-wheeler circuit racing altogether. In 1960, however, the company revived its interest in off-road competition, and Sebastian Nachtmann won gold on his factory R69S in the ISDT at Bad Aussee, Austria.

Despite BMW's absence from the IMF circuit throughout the 1960s, BMW motorsport engineers studied Honda's pioneering, high-revving, "screaming" engines. Many of the incredible design innovations and advancements that evolved in Grand Prix racing in the 1960s would eventually find their way into BMW's production models.

ROCKY ROADS

BMW's R51/3, R67/2, and R68 boxer twins continued to evolve with minor updates, but the single-cylinder R25 series was still by far the top-seller as overall production grew steadily, peaking in 1955. By the mid-1950s, the German economy was rebounding from the war. However, motorcycle sales began to suffer as buyers now aspired to own an automobile.

BMW therefore restarted auto manufacturing in 1952 and did so with a surprisingly deluxe sedan—the 501 "Baroque Angel" with OHV V-8 engine. In 1955, it redesigned the Italian Isetta "bubble" car, installed a 247cc, four-stroke, single-cylinder motorcycle engine, and began producing it as its own. It sold 161,728 that first year! The marque's auto business had finally overtaken its motorcycle business.

Meanwhile, as motorcycle production grew more slowly throughout the early 1950s, BMW had established distribution in Britain. In 1954, it began selling in the United States through New Jersey–based importer Butler & Smith. A BMW's high cost, however, was an impediment. You could buy *two* comparable (and faster) BSAs, Nortons, or Triumphs for the price of a R51/3. Unsurprisingly, sales were disappointing. This, despite BMW finally replacing its pre-war plunger telescopic fork and rear-spring with a full-swing chassis, introduced in 1955 on the 494cc R50 and 594cc R69. The bikes now had a swinging-arm framed Earles fork at the front, while the rear wheel and Cardan shaft were mounted in their own swingarms.

Alas, the release of the R50 and R69 coincided with a collapse in motorcycle sales. Even BMW successes on the race tracks couldn't revive falling demand. As cars became more affordable, BMW's motorcycle production fell to 23,531 in

BMW poster (1956): "Motorcycles matured by more than 25 years of experience."

1955, and then to just 5,429 in 1957, with most bikes now sold to export markets. While motorcycle development and updates stagnated, in 1956 BMW bet badly on the introduction of the striking, yet ultimately expensive and unprofitable, six-cylinder 503 "2+2" *gran turismo* and the even sexier (yet equally expensive and unprofitable) BMW 507 prestige roadster. Losses spiraled. Debts mounted. By the end of 1959, BMW was close to financial ruin. Management planned on selling the company to Daimler-Benz.

Instead, majority shareholder Herbert Quandt (an industrialist who had overseen the use of Nazi slave labor during World War II) increased his stake to 50 percent and restructured the company. BMW's fortunes were now pinned on the 700, a small rear-engine monocoque car based on the Isetta chassis and powered by a fan-cooled 697cc boxer engine. Spacious, lightweight, and with a top speed of 125 km/h (78 mph), it received 25,000 advance orders when introduced as coupe and four-door saloon versions at the 1959 Frankfurt Motor Show. Produced in various models (including a 700 Sport, introduced in 1961) from August 1959 to November 1965, it sold 190,000 units in all, accounting for almost two-thirds of BMW's revenue.

Thereafter, BMW's automotive portfolio grew quickly, dwarfing motorcycle sales (only 8,412 bikes were made in 1959). For the next decade, BMW's motorcycle division languished as a struggling corporate backwater.

BMW R67/3 sidecar outfits of the German Automobile Club's road assistance crew, 1955.

Left The Earles fork had a swinging arm just like at the rear of the BMW and permitted use of similar shock absorbers front and back.

Opposite A factory diagram of the R69S's Earles fork from the 1966 BMW Instruction Manual.

• The Earles Fork

In 1951, English engineer Ernest Earles designed a leading link, light-alloy fork for his BSA 500cc A7 twin. In 1953, he patented his design. The fork was revolutionary for the time, and BMW and MV Agusta licensed it for their racing team motorcycles (MV Agusta also employed it on its 1952 300 Bicilindra prototype, which never went into production). Douglas employed it on its 1955 348cc, opposed-twin Dragonfly. Between 1955 and 1969, BMW licensed the fork for use on all its models, and during the period it became synonymous with the German marque.

The triangulated fork featured two straight tubes that angled down and back from the steering head to behind the front wheel. A pivoting swingarm connected the base of the tubes to the front axle. Two adjustable Boge hydraulic shock absorbers connected the swingarm to the lower fork crown below the steering head. The basis of Earles's patent was that the pivot point was aft of the rear of the front wheel.

The Earles fork was robust and offered greater resistance to lateral deflection during hard cornering, especially when combined (as in BMWs) with a standard swingarm at the rear. Though ponderous in turning, it offered a steady, well-controlled ride and tended not to dive when braking. But, disconcertingly for novice users, it caused the front end to rise during hard braking.

Although it gave idiosyncratic handling on sporting solos, the Earles fork was extremely well-suited to motorcycles hauling sidecars, not least because it could be adjusted for rake and trail. The swinging arm pivot had two sets of holes on the forks: one for solo use, and a lower, forward one for sidecars that reduced the trail angle (and increased the rake) for easier steering.

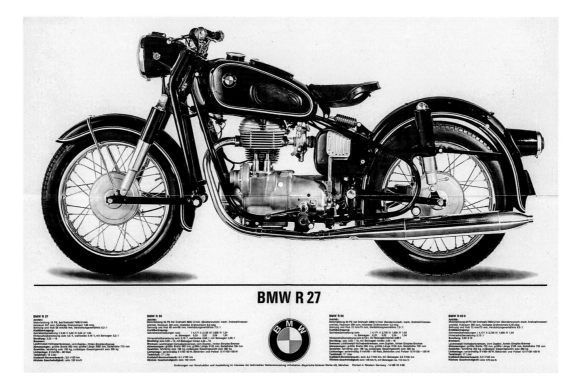

A DECADE IN THE DOLDRUMS

In 1960, BMW presented the R27 as successor to the R26 247cc OHV vertical single. It had a full-swing chassis with triangulated Earles front fork, and the thumper engine was now supported on rubber mounts in the frame to dampen vibrations. While retaining the square bore, the higher 8.2:1 compression plus a larger carburetor (and a more efficient air filter under the seat) boosted power to 18 horsepower. Produced between 1960 and 1966, the R27 would be BMW's last of its engine type, as well as the last single-cylinder motorcycle until introduction of the chain-driven F650 "Funduro" in 1993.

Sectional view of the OHV, pushrod-operated, vertical single-cylinder R27 engine with a cavernous crankcase; the entire unit-construction motor was mounted atop rubber blocks.

SCHLENZIG

Also new in 1960 was the ground-breaking R69S—the fastest German production machine of the era. Displaying the same 594cc as the R69 (1955–1960), its higher compression of 9.5:1 and new Bing carburetors delivered 42 horsepower and a top speed of 175 km/h (107 mph)—enough to rival the racy British Triumph T120 Bonneville. This forerunner to the modern "sport tourer" was also the first BMW motorcycle to get a twin seat and—with an eye on the US market—a choice of paintwork: black or distinctive Dover White ("Alpine White" in the US). It sold well in North America, where *Cycle World* raved, "The R69S is a near perfect machine."

Otherwise, no new models were introduced during the 1960s until the R75 of 1969. The early '60s saw only nominal product updates, with enhancements geared to improving reliability when deemed necessary. BMW bikes were still expensive and (with the exception of the R69S) for the rest of the decade came only in black. Production rose only slightly to 9,460 in 1961, then plunged to just 4,302 in 1962—the lowest since 1927—as BMW focused on expanding car production.

The disappointing R50S was discontinued in 1962, while the R69S's frame and cylinders were reinforced and (for the German market) Hella turn signals were fitted to the handlebar ends. For 1963 and 1964, BMW's entire boxer twin range was unchanged. BMW adopted the status quo with its high-quality yet conservative and increasingly outdated-looking bikes for discerning clients. Annual production remained below 10,000 throughout the mid-1960s.

BMW introduced several mechanical and milquetoast cosmetic updates for 1967, including new carburetors plus redesigned handlebar levers for all models. A new series of US models—R50US, R60US, and R69US—was also unveiled. Each received a new 36mm BMW-designed leading-axle front telescopic fork with gaiter to replace the antiquated-looking Earles fork. Otherwise, the /2 series US models were essentially the same as their European brethren. They garnered relatively little enthusiasm and couldn't prevent a continued slide in demand. Production fell to only 5,074 in 1968, then a dismal 4,701 in 1969.

At the close of the decade, BMW's Earles fork boxer twins still resembled the bikes of 1960. Compared to the competition, they now looked antiquated and ungainly. Plus, except for the R69S, performance was sedate. And the bikes, with their lavish attention to refinement and finish, were expensive to produce. Once again, the viability of BMW's now-unprofitable motorcycle division was in jeopardy.

In May 1969, with BMW's automobile division increasingly profitable, the company relocated motorcycle production to a new factory in Berlin to make way for expanded auto production in Munich. The change would prove beneficial. Exciting new motorcycles—the /5 series—with an all-new boxer engine were in the works. They would represent a whole new style shift—and a BMW motorcycle renaissance.

R 27 Touren-Sport 250 ccm 18 PS

R 50 Touren-Sport 500 ccm 26 PS

...so gut wie sie aus sehen

R 50 S Sport 500 ccm 35 PS

R 60 Touren-Sport 600 ccm 30 PS

R 69 S Sport 600 ccm 42 PS

"BMW ... as good as they look!" proclaims this 1960 advertisement
featuring the R27 Sports Tourer, R50 Sports Tourer, R50S Sport,
R60 Sports Tourer, and R69S Sport.

• Steib Sidecars

Almost from its inception, BMW designed motorcycles for use with sidecars at a time when they were popular modes of family transport. Almost all BMW motorcycles came with three-point attachment points built into the frame. Many models—notably the R60 and the R67 series (which came with two sets of gearbox ratios, one for solo use and the second for sidecars)—were specifically intended for hauling sidecars built to BMW's specifications by Josef Steib Spezialfabrik für Seitenwagen of Nuremnberg. Although Steib made several designs, its most iconic versions were BMW's own specially commissioned Spezial model based on the TR500 with customized trim and the iconic Zeppelin-like S350 Standard.

Steib's seitenwagens were as functional as they were stylish. The Art Deco–inspired, bullet-shaped Standard had a very thin metal "boat" (body) and leather seat, and weighed only about 45 kg (100 lbs). It was painted in BMW's trademark gloss black with white pinstripes, and featured a sturdy chrome crashbar and trim.

The Earles fork that became synonymous with BMW models between 1955 and 1969 was perfectly suited for use with sidecar rigs. But its introduction coincided with a decline in sidecar sales, as the rise in automobile sales effectively killed the market. Steib, once the major sidecar producer in Europe, ceased production in 1958.

R75

When World War II broke out, the German army was already heavily invested in motorcycle sidecar combos, which it used for primary transportation. The Wehrmacht's three-wheel workhorse was the military-spec R12, which BMW had been selling since it introduced the 745cc side-valve R12 in 1935. In 1937, the army requested that BMW and its competitor, Zündapp, each design a new 750cc sidecar rig to military specifications. The new purpose-built, cross-country vehicles had to have a minimum ground clearance of 150cm (59in), sustain a "marching speed" of 4 km/h (2.5 mph) without overheating, and maintain 80 km/h (50 mph) with a payload of 500 kg (1,102 lbs)—equivalent to more than half a ton!

BMW's answer—the bulletproof R75—was capable of all this, and more. Designed by engineer and racing driver Alex von Falkenhausen and chief engineer Rudolf Schleicher, the most complex BMW motorcycle yet built was powered by a 748cc OHV engine derived from the R71's side-valve design with a square 78mm x 78mm bore and stroke.

Twin Graetzin Sa24 carburetors fed the engine through a triple air-filter system initially positioned above the gearbox but relocated in 1942 to beneath a helmet-like cover atop the fuel tank. That year, R75s serving in Rommel's Afrika Korps got a fan-cooled engine.

The R75's low 5.8:1 compression allowed the grunty engine to burn extremely low-octane fuel, yet still produced 26 horsepower, a top speed of 98 km/h (60 mph), and ample torque to power through mud and sand. The ingenious transmission featured shaft drive to both rear and sidecar wheels and incorporated a sophisticated power-dividing crown wheel differential that applied unequal torque to each wheel on their stub axles. A limited-slip differential could be locked into tandem drive when conditions became really tough.

The four-speed transmission for on-road use featured a dog clutch, plus four low-ratio speeds for off-road, and two reverse gears, operated by both hand- and foot-shift levers.

1941

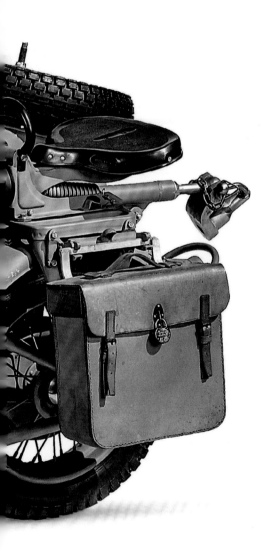

With wide, interchangeable wheels shod with knobby tires (plus tire-chains for snowy conditions), the R75 could negotiate more or less any surface. The 16in (41.6cm) wheels were interchangeable with those of the Wehrmacht's Kübelwagen. BMW gave the R75 a strengthened, double-action, hydraulic telescopic front fork (the rear end was rigid). This behemoth Beemer needed all the stopping power it could muster, so both rear wheels were fitted with foot-pedal hydraulic drum brakes while a mechanical drum served at the front.

The motor was mounted in a bolted tubular steel frame with a split in the lower spars that made it easy for the engine to be quickly removed and reinstalled. Nonetheless, although astoundingly reliable and requiring little maintenance, the R75 was expensive to build, as well as complicated. It was considered inferior to Zündapp's robust KS750 powered by an air-cooled, 170-degree 751cc boxer engine.

R24

Opposite Sectional drawing of the R24's four-speed gearbox.

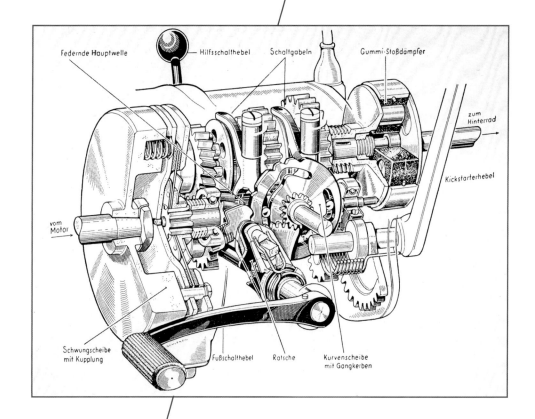

Federnde Hauptwelle — Hilfsschalthebel — Schaltgabeln — Gummi-Stoßdämpfer

zum Hinterrad

Kickstarterhebel

vom Motor

Schwungscheibe mit Kupplung — Fußschalthebel — Ratsche — Kurvenscheibe mit Gangkerben

1948

After World War II ended, BMW applied what little money it had to rebuilding the Munich factory. With limited funds left over for motorcycle development, in common with almost all surviving motorcycle and automobile manufacturers, the company started production by rehashing one or more pre-war models. Thus, in 1948, BMW released the R24 (a near carbon copy of the R23), developed by dismantling and reverse engineering an existing R23 to create new blueprints because the originals had been destroyed (or appropriated by the Soviets) in the war.

The 247cc single-cylinder OHV engine (named the 224/I) retained a perfectly square 68mm x 68mm bore and stroke, with the cylinder set vertically on an alloy crankcase and still fed by a 22mm Bing type AJ carburetor. Nonetheless, the engine was upgraded with significant improvements, including a new cylinder head (with pushrods inserted through tunnels) and two-piece valve covers, all based on those of the wartime R75. Valve angles were altered for better performance, and the compression raised to a still modest 6.75:1, upping horsepower two ponies to 23hp at 5,600rpm. This was good for a top speed of 100 km/h (62 mph). BMW also added a fourth gear—a first for its single-cylinder engines.

Of course, the R24 retained BMW's trademark shaft drive, but it now incorporated a cush-drive assembly on the end of the crankshaft to spread the drive load during hard acceleration or braking. The 121 kg (268 lbs) bike was stopped by 160mm (6.3in) drum brakes to front and rear.

The R24 inherited the R23's rigid twin-cradle tubular frame of bolted-together pressed-steel sections, as well as an undampened telescopic front fork. There was still no rear suspension (that would appear on the R24's replacement, the R25, in 1950). But a distinctive left-side black-painted (yet subsequently chromed) fishtail muffler and white trim edging the gas tank and fenders added a little class to the bike.

As German society began to recover from the devastating war years, buyers were clamoring for inexpensive mobility. The simple and reliable R24 symbolized a new dawn and proved particularly popular with the German police. Although several German competitors offered less expensive, smaller displacement motorcycles (from the NSU Fox with a 98cc four-stroke engine and the two-stroke DKW RT 125 to the 500cc Horex Imperator parallel twin), BMW's R24 was the stand-out option. More than 9,000 were sold in 1949, helping consolidate BMW's renaissance. Production extended through May 1950, when the R24 was replaced by the R25.

R51/2

Fahrkomfort

durch Allradfederung **BMW**

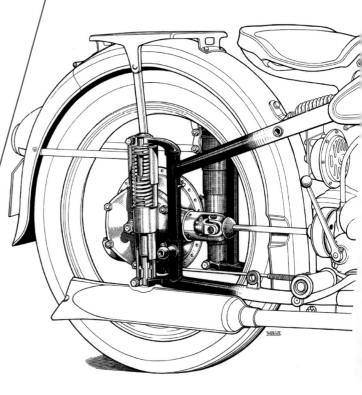

Left "Driving comfort thanks to all-wheel suspension" boasts this BMW advertisement for the R51/2.

Above R51/2s began to roll off the production line in Munich in 1950.

Right Cutaway of the R51/2's plunger rear-wheel suspension inherited from the pre-war R51, R61, R66, and R71.

R 51/2

In the summer of 1950, the American occupying forces lifted the restriction on production of motorcycles above 250cc. As for the R24, BMW engineers tore down surviving pre-war R51 motorcycles and using the measurements for every component, rebuilt and revised it as the R51/2.

The original 494cc OHV machine was state-of-the-art when launched in 1938. BMW updated the chassis and engine and confidently presented the new 500cc-class boxer twin in March 1950 at the Geneva International Motor Show, and that August at the Chicago Trade Fair.

Visually, little distinguished the R51/2 from its progenitor. It used the same electrically welded, oval-section tubular steel frame, but with two additional strengthening tubes. And the front telescopic fork now had two-way hydraulic damping. The R51/2's engine was also virtually identical to the original pre-war motor, except for new cylinder heads that now had coil valve springs, plus split valve covers (echoing those of the R75) and a coil-spring damper on the gearbox mainshaft. Twin 22mm Bing Spezial carburetors replaced the Amals. And a revised lubrication system improved flow of pressured oil to the camshaft bearings and cylinder heads.

As with all boxer tourers, the R51 frame featured attachment points that permitted sidecar use. The R51/2 proved popular when fitted with Steib's eye-catching, single-seat, Zeppelin-like Standard sidecar built to BMW's specifications with a leather-covered passenger compartment and full windscreen. From almost the company's very founding, BMW built sturdy, black side-rigs suited to their torquey, low-compression twin-cylinder tourers.

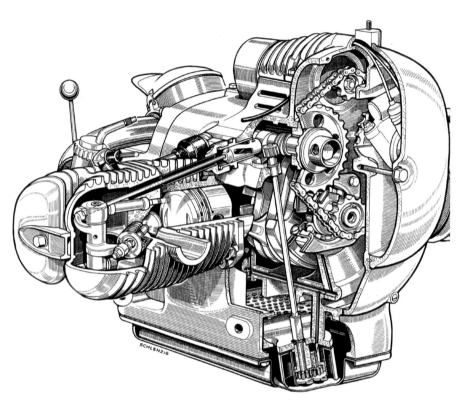

BMW engineers quickly improved on the stop-gap R51/2, which sold more than 5,000 before being replaced the following year by the greatly enhanced R51/3 sports model. Although aesthetically an identical twin to the R51/2, the third-generation model had an all-new engine enclosed in a narrower, more modern-looking engine case featuring clean new rocker covers replacing the former two-piece valve covers. A single camshaft driven by helical gears now controlled the valves via pushrods that ran from the top of the crankshaft, eliminating the R51/2's long timing chain. The cylinders, heads, and five-ring pistons were also new. A Norris magneto now provided the spark instead of the prior coil ignition. A cigar-shaped muffler relaced the fishtail. And a new intake design atop the transmission featured a paper-based Knecht air filter. Despite these, and other, improvements, power remained unchanged at 24 horsepower, giving a top speed of 140 km/h (87 mph).

Further changes were made annually until the R51/3 was replaced by the R50 with full-swing suspension in 1955.

Opposite Sectional drawing of the R51/2's single-cam, twin-carb OHV engine with split valve covers, coil valve springs, and coil-spring damper on the gearbox mainshaft.

Above The torquey, low-compression R51/2 was popular as a sidecar-rig wed to the Steib Standard.

R68

Although BMW produced perhaps the finest 500cc-category bikes of the time, it lacked a more muscular sports model capable of challenging the British BSA and Triumph 650cc twins that were preeminent in their class (especially in the US, the top export market). BMW engineers therefore developed a new higher performance sportster styled on the factory team's race machines. The much-anticipated 594cc R68—BMW's first 161 km/h (100 mph) production motorcycle—debuted at the Motor Show in October 1951.

The company's new sporting flagship, nicknamed the "100 Mile Racer," was priced at almost 4,000 Deutsch Marks, well beyond the reach of the average buyer. BMW sold only 1,452 R68s between 1952 and 1954. But the first true "Sportsmodell" since the R66 solidified the company's post-war stature for building high-performance engines and seriously competitive sport bikes.

BMW used the mild-mannered R67/2's chassis. Hinting at the R68's sporty character, however, were a narrower and more modern front-wheel mudguard plus optional elevated exhaust system and sprung pillion pad with a chrome grab handle (the pillion was integrated into the saddle to permit riders to slide back for a more prone racing posture). Although the show model featured upswept two-in-one exhausts first seen on the factory R51/3 racers, the production R68 had standard low-level fishtail pipes.

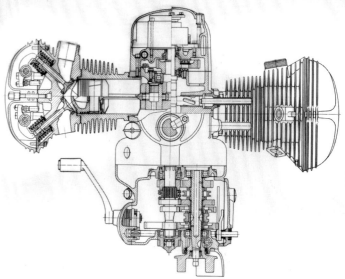

Above *Female Belgian journalist Marianne Weber puts the 1952 R68 through its paces for a test report.*
Right *This plan drawing of the R68's 594cc OHV engine shows the horizontally offset opposed-twin cylinders.*

Evolved from the low-compression R67/2, the enhanced engine had a power output of 35 horsepower thanks to 8.0:1 high-compression pistons, larger valves, larger 26mm Bing carburetors, restyled twin-rib valve covers, a racing-type magneto, and a more aggressive high-performance cam profile. BMW engineers also added a manual spark control lever to the handlebar clutch control. Finally, BMW had a model that could keep up with such comparable British twins as the 1952 Triumph Thunderbird 6T (Marlon Brando's rebel rousing ride in the 1953 film *The Wild One*).

The 200mm (7.9in) drum brakes were inherited from the R51/3A, but the improved duplex leading-shoe offered greater braking power. In 1952, rubber gaiters were added to the telescopic front fork (the rear suspension was an archaic short-travel plunger rear), and torpedo-type mufflers replaced the fishtails. For 1953, the frame was given a sidecar mount and full-width aluminum-alloy hubs and wheel rims, which were introduced across the entire BMW range. Changes for 1954 included a larger headlamp and enhanced front brake.

With stellar performance for its day, the R68 is rightly considered among the most impressive of BMW's post-war motorcycles, and it re-established the company's reputation for refined, high-performance production machines. It lasted until 1960, when it handed over the laurels as the most powerful BMW post-war production model to the R69S.

R25/3

When in 1951 BMW revealed the single-cylinder R25/2 as successor to the R25 (launched the prior year and still bearing the imprimatur of the pre-war R23), its changes were merely cosmetic. By contrast, although visually still clearly half a boxer twin (same cylinder and head, valve gear, and so on), the third generation R25/3 was significantly upgraded. Intended originally for military, police, and postal duty, it was an all-around better motorcycle and would become the most successful BMW motorcycle to date, with 47,700 built (about half went to service work; half sold to the public).

The most notable difference was its redesigned, flatter, and longer fuel tank with a lockable left-side toolbox replacing the R52/2's top-of-tank toolbox. The lower and leaner /3 also gained improved suspension thanks to manual front-fork hydraulic damping and increased travel, and the plunger-style rear suspension first introduced on the R25. Also new were lightweight alloy wheel rims and full-width alloy hubs with a single-leading shoe drum brake.

1953/55

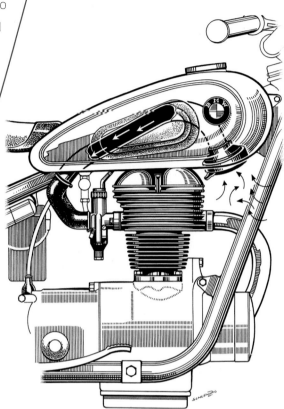

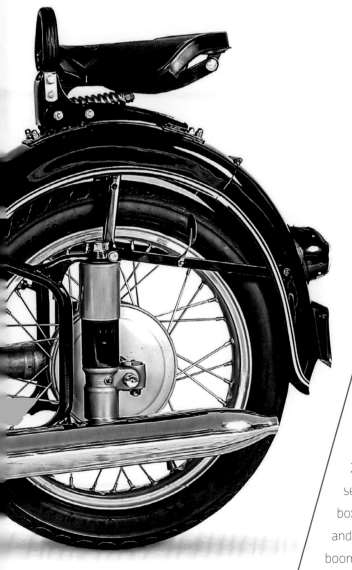

A new welded steel twin-loop tubular frame cusped a moderately upgraded engine, now with a 7:1 compression ratio (up from 6.5:1) that increased output to 13 horsepower at 5,800rpm. A larger 24mm Bing carburetor with new, longer air intake improved fuel delivery and breathing and helped increase midrange torque (BMW had learned how to maximize power by tuning induction tracts on its aero engines during World War II). The slight power increase could now propel bike and rider to 120 km/h (74 mph), impressive for a 247cc single! A black-painted cylinder head improved heat dissipation.

Power to the four-speed gearbox was via a single-plate clutch. True to most BMWs of the day, the first three gears were relatively close, with the more-distant fourth serving as a kind of overdrive.

A small-bore study in class and utility, it was the right model at the right time. Although BMW had introduced the 500cc R51/2 in 1949, the 247cc model was the company's bread and butter and sold twice as fast, securing BMW's future and funding the next generation of singles and boxers. In 1956, it was replaced by the R26 featuring the Earles fork front and swingarm rear suspension. However, the post-war small-motorcycle boom was fading. Neither the R26 or subsequent R27 sold anywhere near as well as the R25/3. The last BMW 250cc single was built in 1968.

R60/R60/2

By 1955, BMW's frame with rudimentary telescopic front fork and plunger rear suspension was considered archaic. BMW's RS255 Kompressor and Rennsport RS54 racing machines were already winning trophies with state-of-the-art front-end Earles fork and rear swingarm suspension. In January 1958, BMW turned its back on the past and introduced two new boxer models—the R50 and the R69—based on the innovative full-swing chassis (named the 245/1). They were followed in April 1956 by the utility-model, full-swing-chassis R60 tourer, intended to replace the R67 as the company's sidecar-combo model.

The R60 visually was a carbon copy of the R50, but with an upgraded version of the R67/3's robust 594cc, 28-horsepower engine, which produced the enormous yet smooth torque and gentle power delivery necessary to move the bike and sidecar. It also had a higher rear-wheel ratio than its R50 and R69 siblings, lending further to its credentials for leisurely touring. Even without a sidecar, it needed a slight downhill incline or strong tailwind to top 145 km/h (90 mph).

Not that the R50 and R69 were thrilling performers. The former was powered by the R51/3's previous generation 494cc engine with new pistons and a slight increase in compression; the more sporting R69 utilized the R68's marginally upgraded 594cc, 35-horsepower mill.

The new models' launch coincided with the mid-1950s implosion in motorcycle sales. Several German motorcycle manufacturers had filed for bankruptcy, and dark clouds shadowed the 1960 Cologne International Bicycle and Motorcycle Exhibition. Herbert Quandt's investment in BMW, however, had financed significant improvements to the boxer lineup, relaunched in Cologne as the R50/2 and R60/2 tourers and R50S and R69S sportsters. Both tourers were upgraded with stronger bearings and crankshafts, while the R60/2 received high-compression pistons and an increase in compression (from 6.5:1 to 7.5:1) that boosted output to 30 horsepower at 5,800rpm.

Europeans of the 1950s were still in recovery mode after World War II, and both the R50S and R60/2 gave them the reliability and sound economy that, above all, they sought in a motorcycle. The models sold particularly well with motorized police divisions and commercial fleets. With minimal annual updates, they survived a decade of remarkable longevity until an entire new generation appeared in 1969. By then, the Earles fork setup was itself considered obsolete. In 1967, the US version of the R50/2, R60/2, and R69S were given a sophisticated leading axle telescopic fork in lieu of the Earles fork.

1953/55

The utilitarian R60 featured elegant Hella turn signals fitted to the handlebar ends.

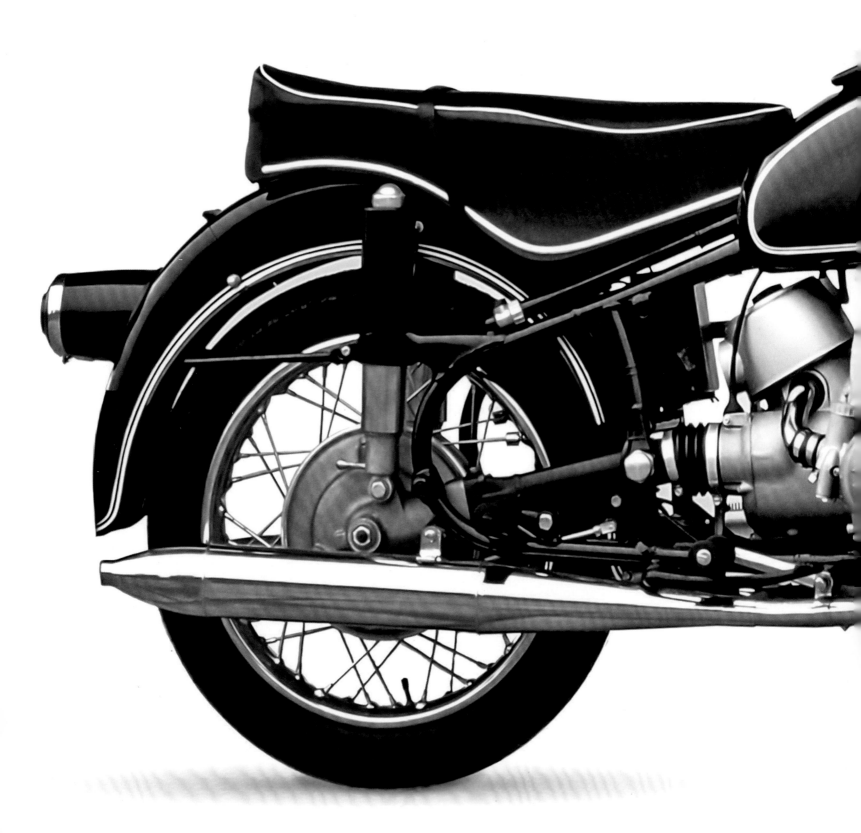

Fitted with the Earles fork, the full-swing-chassis R60/2 (like its predecessor) was designed as a utility tourer and flagship sidecar-combo model.

R69S

BMW's flagship sporting motorcycle, the R68 of 1951, had grown long in the tooth by the close of the decade. BMW engineers understood that the chassis's capabilities were at their limit for its robust engine. Its replacement—the R69S—could top 175 km/h (109 mph), setting a new benchmark as the most powerful and fastest production BMW twin yet. The newcomer, however, launched in 1960, when BMW and its German competitors were once again struggling to stay solvent.

Essentially an updated and steroid-enhanced version of the R69, its higher-performance engine had new three-ring pistons that ran at a significantly higher 9.5:1 compression, and new Bing carburetors fed larger inlet ports. These combined with stronger internals (among them a larger air filter, a rotary disc crankcase ventilator, a strengthened spherical roller bearing, a gear-driven camshaft, and a harmonic balancer on the built-up crankshaft) and a larger diameter exhaust to deliver 42 horsepower at 7,000rpm.

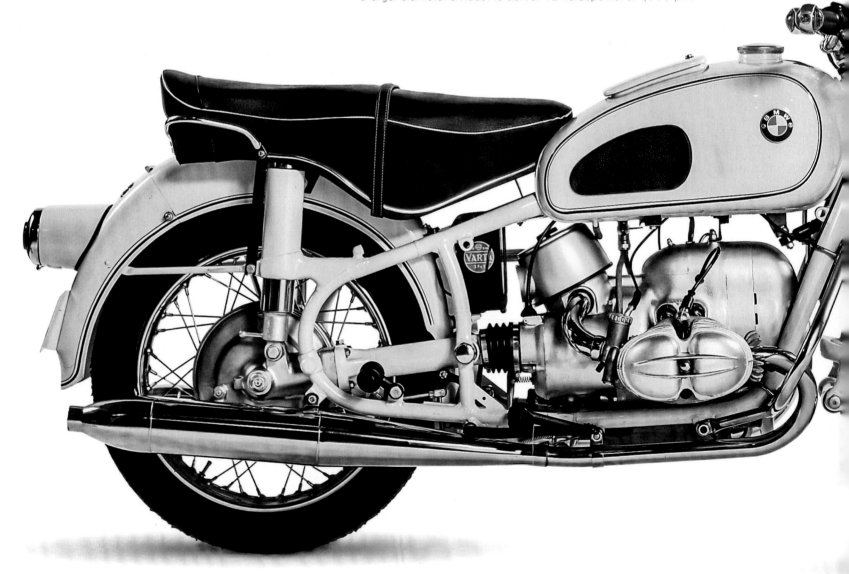

Right Sectional cutaway of the R69S's superbly engineered motor with gear-driven camshaft, large inlet ports, and oversize air filter.

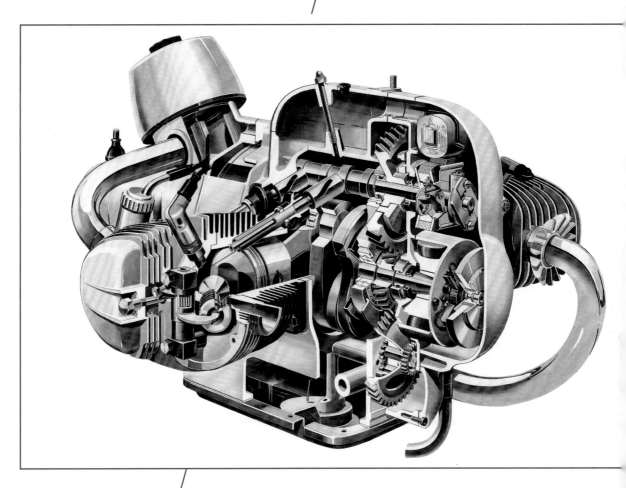

Although considered a sublime piece of engineering, the S-model engine at first suffered substantial problems, not least of which were crankshaft flex and a tendency for engine failure after long runs at high revs.

The engine was bolted to a frame derived from the Rennsport RS54 racer with the same full-swing suspension already featured on the R50, R60, and R69. However, the R69S (and its smaller cousin, the R50S) featured a hydraulic steering damper—activated by a knob on the steering head—to tame unsettling headshake created by the Earles fork's unsprung weight. The new full-swing suspension with damper dramatically improved the bike's comfort, control, and handling, even when ridden aggressively.

BMW's stylists tried to set the R69S apart visually by giving it a somewhat bulky dual seat and optional Dover White paintwork (and, in the US, Dominican Blue-Gray, Macaw Green, or Granada Red by special order). You could even order a larger gas tank, a single seat, crash bars, a special fairing, plus a tachometer (which as yet no BMW production bike featured).

The R69S enjoyed a 10-year lifespan (1960–1969) with yearly updates: among them reinforced cylinders in 1962; rubber-mounted vibration dampers on the crankshaft and reinforced springs to cure clutch slip in 1964; and for the US models, new telescopic forks to replace the by-now-ungainly outdated Earles fork.

The R69S was the most popular BMW model in America, despite being comparatively expensive. It represented the peak of quintessential BMW style and performance to date. "For long-distance, high-speed touring, there is no better motorcycle on earth," raved *Cyclist* magazine. In all, 11,317 of the flagship model were sold before styles changed dramatically in the 1970s, taking BMW in entirely new directions.

1969

1982

A NEW BOXER GENERATION

A NEW GENERATION

In May 1969, BMW relocated motorcycle manufacturing to a former Siemens aircraft engine factory in Spandau, on the outskirts of West Berlin. It marked a major reset for a company whose motorcycles had metaphorically stalled. The motorcycle market had shifted gears dramatically in the 1960s. Japanese manufacturers had introduced stylish large-displacement machines that now dominated the race circuit and the consumer market with their power, reliability, and sophistication.

By comparison, and notwithstanding that BMW motorcycles incorporated modern advanced technology, the German bikes looked very outdated with their stodgy pre-war styling. BMW dealers were finding their bikes a hard sell. BMW's technical director Helmut Werner Bönsch and motorcycle operations chief Wilfried Kramm understood that after a decade of evolutionary stagnation, the company needed to develop a whole new generation of luxury motorcycles with aggressively contemporary styling.

The /5 series—the R50/5, R60/5, and R75/5—unveiled in the fall of 1969 was a radical shift for BMW. Although incorporating the classic boxer-twin layout, motorcycle development manager (and racer) Hans-Günther von der Marwitz wanted the new bikes to combine a plush ride with the handling of a Manx Norton production racer. He disliked the "pendulum" Earles fork and '60s chassis that harked back to the early BMW rigid frame. Inspired by the Norton "featherbed" double-cradle frame, the /5 series frame featured variable section tubing and a bolted-on rear subframe designed exclusively for solo riding. It comprised a true clean-sheet design and corrected many of the prior generation frame's shortcomings (although the rear subframe was a weak link).

The /5 series models were powered by all-new boxer engines that shared the same architecture and employed the same 70.6mm stroke with variable cylinder bores to achieve the 498cc, 599cc, and 745cc displacements. The engine was a vast improvement on the earlier /2 series mill. An aluminum one-piece reinforced tunnel-housing enclosed a one-piece forged crankshaft, with the camshaft now under the engine and driven from the crank by a duplex chain. An electric starter motor (optional on the R50/5) with battery and coil ignition replaced the earlier magneto. And a brand-new air-intake system incorporated an oversize rear-facing air-intake grille, with the air filter inside the engine case.

The /5s also featured a Fichtel & Sachs leading-axle telescopic fork (first introduced on the /2US series), twin Boge shock absorbers at the rear, and a capacious and comfy scalloped dual seat. A large trapezoidal 24-liter (6.35-gallon) fuel tank was now offered in red, blue, white, and chrome, with matching fiberglass fenders, as well as traditional gloss black. The /5 series' new four-speed gearbox improved on BMW's famously clunky shift but required multiple modifications in ensuing years. And the early /5 bikes suffered unnerving high-speed "head shake" (front-end wobble). This was finally resolved in 1973 when engineers lengthened the wheelbase and swingarm.

Despite these niggling problems, the /5s provided better handling than any previous BMW motorcycle, as well as unparalleled touring comfort and BMW's trademark reliability. The bikes looked good, handled well, and delivered sporty performance. The motorcycling press raved about their all-encompassing refinement, which revolutionized BMW's motorcycling image, made them competitive with the Japanese, and destined the /5 series to become one of BMW's top success stories. In 1970, riders bought 12,346 of the /5 series (the strongest BMW motorcycle sales since 1955), then 18,898 the following year, vindicating Bönsch's faith in the new generation model. During its four-year lifespan, 68,956 rolled off the production line, with the last /5s leaving the Spandau factory on July 28, 1973, just three days after the 500,000th BMW motorcycle had been produced.

Above left *Aerial view of BMW's new manufacturing plant in Spandau, Berlin, where production began in May 1969.*

Above right *The R60/5 boasted an eye-pleasing contemporary design, with a leading-axle telescopic fork replacing the Earles fork.*

Opposite *Steve McLaughlin (83) and Reg Pridmore (163) battle it out on their BMW R90Ss to take gold and silver, respectively, at the first-ever AMA Superbike race in Daytona, Florida.*

CAFÉ RACER SUPREME

In 1973, BMW significantly updated its R60 and R75 and released them as the /6 series (now minus the slow-selling 500cc model) with new closer-ratio five-speed transmission and, for the R75/6, a long over-due single-disc front brake. The series also included the R90/6—a long-anticipated "sportmodell" with the /6 series engine bored out to 898cc for a prodigious 60 horsepower at 6,500rpm and a top speed of 185 km/h (115 mph).

In 1969, Honda had astonished the motorcycling world (and rewritten the rulebook) with its affordable, ultra-reliable, four-cylinder, 67-horsepower CB750. BMW's answer to this Japanese superbike was the equally momentous R90S, unveiled in 1974. The company's most powerful motorcycle yet, BMW's new flagship superbike used a performance-tuned, high compression (9.5:1) version of the R90/6 engine with 90mm bore and accelerator-pump 38mm (1.5in) Dellorto carburetors. It pumped out 67 horsepower and with its top speed of almost 200 km/h (124 mph) for the first time ever in a BMW production machine, provided class-leading performance equal to the CB750 and any other motorcycle then in production.

Equally eye-popping was the R90S's stunning styling. BMW designer Hans Muth set a new standard for the entire motorcycle industry with his iconic, cutting-edge café-racer design featuring a swept-back bikini fairing, svelte 24L (6.3 gallon) gas tank, sporty tapered "ducktail" rear end, and beautiful two-tone misted metallic Silver Smoke finish (and Daytona Orange in 1975). The suspension, too, was state-of-the-art. The R90S's long-travel front telescopic front forks and twin rear shocks with pre-load dampers tamed rough pavement and delivered sporty handling, while a hydraulic steering damper with adjuster atop the steering head enhanced cornering stability. Its dual-vented front disc brakes could stop the bike on a dime.

The R90S vanquished BMW's conservative image for producing reliable and durable, yet staid and uti-litarian bikes. Suddenly, BMW was elevated to the sporting motorcycle limelight. The timing was perfect: sportiness was now in demand and motorcycle consumers considered sharp design and raw power more important than ever.

The R90S could actually speed ahead of the exotic 82-horsepower, 900cc Kawasaki Zl *and* the Honda CB750. (Its status as a giant-killer was confirmed in 1976 when the R90S took gold and silver in the first-ever AMA Superbike race in Daytona.) Plus, a rider could cruise all day at 160 km/h (100 mph) in comfort. No other bike of the time combined such reliability, performance, handling, comfort, and great styling. One of the best-looking bikes ever built, the glamorous and fast R90S even came with integrated luggage cases and a comfy dual seat, and was the first genuine "sport tourer."

It was also expensive. Selling in the US for a manufacturer's suggested retail price (MSRP) of $3,800—the equivalent in today's money of about $30,000, and three times the price of a Triumph Bonneville—it nonetheless was a massive success. Almost 17,500 were sold before the end of production in 1976.

The /6 series motorcycles were improved year by year, selling more than 25,000 in 1975, when all models got the R90S's five-speed transmission and perforated front disc brake. For 1976, the bikes were given the R90S's stronger engine housing and new cylinders, and cylinder heads with new rockers; 28,209 /6 series motorcycles were sold. In 1977, they received bored-out cylinders and were renamed the /7 series: the R75 became the R80/7 (798 cc) and the R90/6 became the R100/7 (980 cc). The R90S was replaced by the look-alike R100S. But the latter had less horsepower and was no longer issued in the hypnotic misty metallic paint job. It didn't sell well.

Unveiled in 1974, the 60hp R90/6 "sportmodell" could attain 185 km/h (115 mph) and, along with the R75/6, was the first BMW production motorcycle with a front disk brake.

Above BMW utilized Pininfarina's wind-tunnel testing to develop the full and vented wraparound fairing for the R100RS sport tourer.

Opposite The elegant fully dressed R100RT Reisetourer came with a wraparound fairing, large windscreen, and twin panniers.

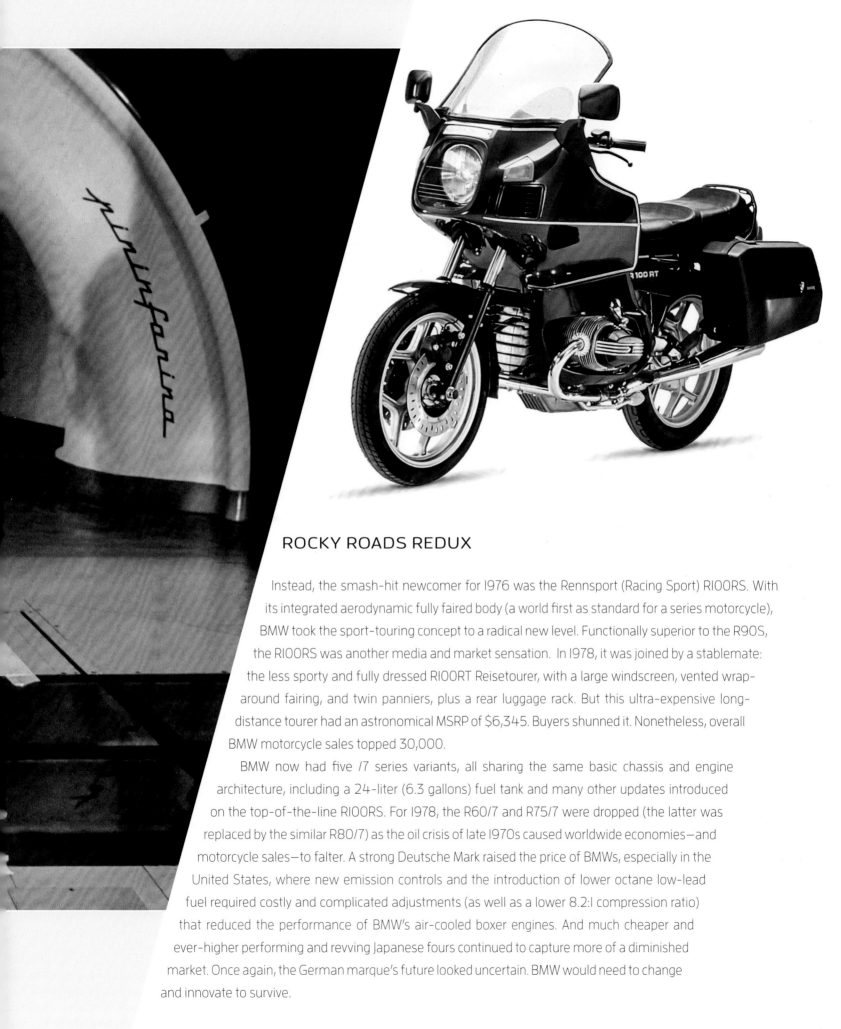

ROCKY ROADS REDUX

Instead, the smash-hit newcomer for 1976 was the Rennsport (Racing Sport) R100RS. With its integrated aerodynamic fully faired body (a world first as standard for a series motorcycle), BMW took the sport-touring concept to a radical new level. Functionally superior to the R90S, the R100RS was another media and market sensation. In 1978, it was joined by a stablemate: the less sporty and fully dressed R100RT Reisetourer, with a large windscreen, vented wrap-around fairing, and twin panniers, plus a rear luggage rack. But this ultra-expensive long-distance tourer had an astronomical MSRP of $6,345. Buyers shunned it. Nonetheless, overall BMW motorcycle sales topped 30,000.

BMW now had five /7 series variants, all sharing the same basic chassis and engine architecture, including a 24-liter (6.3 gallons) fuel tank and many other updates introduced on the top-of-the-line R100RS. For 1978, the R60/7 and R75/7 were dropped (the latter was replaced by the similar R80/7) as the oil crisis of late 1970s caused worldwide economies—and motorcycle sales—to falter. A strong Deutsche Mark raised the price of BMWs, especially in the United States, where new emission controls and the introduction of lower octane low-lead fuel required costly and complicated adjustments (as well as a lower 8.2:1 compression ratio) that reduced the performance of BMW's air-cooled boxer engines. And much cheaper and ever-higher performing and revving Japanese fours continued to capture more of a diminished market. Once again, the German marque's future looked uncertain. BMW would need to change and innovate to survive.

In 1979, a new motorcycle division management team took over under Karl Heinz Gerlinger, with engineers and designers drafted from its automotive division. Gerlinger's brief was simple: reverse the *motorrad* division's waning fortunes or close it down. That year, the 1,000cc twin range was expanded to five models, all powered by the updated high-output "S" engine with 40mm Bing carbs. Two new, smaller short-stroke boxer twins—the R45 and R65—were also released in the hope of widening BMW's appeal. Narrower and in many regards better handling than their similar yet larger siblings, they were relatively anemic and never struck a chord with potential buyers. This was

Above *The R60/7 was the smallest BMW motorcycle between 1973 and 1978, and shared the same 24-liter (6.3 gallons) fuel tank and basic chassis and engine architecture as its four /7 series siblings.*

especially true in the US (which now accounted for one-third of BMW sales), where the falling dollar had also raised the cost of the R100RT to an astronomical $7,195!

Meanwhile, the new design team began developing an entirely new range of motorcycle—the water-cooled, in-line-powered K-series, which would launch in 1984. But BMW wasn't giving up on the boxer. In fact, 1980 saw perhaps the most seminal moment in the company's evolution when it introduced what would become its most successful series ever: the G/S.

Above A consummate touring machine, the R75/7 combined impressive performance with gorgeous looks, courtesy of its R90S-style fuel tank.

GS ADVENTURE TOURERS

In 1979, BMW rider Rolf Witthöft won the prestigious International Six Day Trials (ISDT) in Seigen, West Germany, using a purpose-built, 872cc, boxer-twin-powered, race-only GS80 trail bike. Featuring a special chassis with a monoshock rear suspension, this off-road behemoth weighed a relatively light 135 kg (298 lbs). BMW had a production 798cc R80G/S (shorthand for Geländ/Strasse; "off-road/street") in showrooms the following year. The company had birthed the "adventure-tourer" genre of motorcycle, aimed at the adventurer rider and long-distance explorer.

Although too heavy for pure dedicated off-road riding, the milestone all-purpose "dual-sport" motorcycle was light and nimble for a big-engine bike and displayed excellent street and off-street behavior. Most radical was its sophisticated, all-new rear suspension. The driveshaft was integrated with the right-side Monolever rear swingarm and monoshock setup as a single unit. At the front, the telescopic fork had longer suspension travel and a large 53.3cm (21in) front wheel. And a two-into-one exhaust allowed the pipes to be mounted above and clear of the suspension. The R80G/S debuted at the Cologne Motorcycle Show in the autumn of 1980. It quickly became the top-selling bike in the BMW lineup, accounting for more than one in five BMW sales in its first year. BMW's engineers had pulled a rabbit out of the hat. Sales were further boosted by spectacular first-, fourth-, and seventh-place wins in the 1981 Paris-Dakar Rally.

• Paris-Dakar

In 1977, French motorcycle racer Thierry Sabine conceived a race from Paris to Dakar (Senegal) via the Sahara Desert as the world's toughest off-road endurance event. The inaugural 10,000km (6,200-mile) race took place in 1979 with 182 competitors.

"Win on Sunday, sell on Monday" had been a guiding principle of BMW since it began building motorcycles in 1923. The youthful company understood that motorcycles that won competitive races earned their street credentials with the buying public. Thus, it was no surprise when in 1980—the year of the R80G/S's public debut—BMW Motorrad entered two factory machines in the grueling rally, with Frenchman Jean-Claude Morellet riding his 798cc BMW R80G/S (modified and made "desert-proof" by German off-road specialist HPN) to a fifth-place finish.

In 1981, Frenchman Hubert Auriol crossed the finish line first, launching the R80G/S to fame. Auriol repeated his victory two years later on a G/S bored to 980cc. Then, in 1984, the BMW works team dominated the event, with three-time world motocross champion Gaston Rahier taking first, Auriol coming in second, and Raymond Loizeaux coming in fifth. BMW followed that up in 1985 when Rahier again powered a 75-horsepower boxer through sand, dust, heat, and cold to cross the finish line first in Lac Rose, Dakar.

BMW Motorrad celebrated the victories by producing a 1985-only limited edition R80G/S Paris-Dakar production model with a 32-liter (8.4 gallon) gas tank. Meanwhile, sales of the R80G/S skyrocketed to their own victory.

The R80ST was a street-oriented sibling based on the R80G/S, but with smaller, more street-friendly 19-inch wheels, plus shorter handlebars, forks, and suspension travel.

The advent of the K series would soon sound the death knell for BMW's 1,000cc boxer twins. The R80G/S was the only boxer to survive intact, becoming the inspiration and mold for the last series of air-head twins. Meanwhile, the 1981 R100 series (with four models: the R100, R100RT, R100RS, and R100CS replacing the R100S) got the improved 70-horsepower AIO boxer engine plus an upgraded Bosch electronic system, including electronic ignition. The sporty cockpit-faired R100CS was now the fastest BMW motorcycle of its time, with a top speed of 200 km/h (124 mph). Many of the improvements to the R100 series were carried over to the competent (yet still underpowered and expensive) 1981 model year R45 and R65 middleweights.

The boxer twins received few changes for 1982 as BMW focused its resources on developing the K series. But a new and racier-looking model—the controversial R65LS—was introduced. Its sharp-angled, fork-mounted spoiler, radical composite cast wheels, plus black-painted exhaust and garish color scheme seemed ostentatious. By BMW standards, it seemed a bit of a cheap "parts bin special." The entry-level bike flopped with consumers. The pricey road-going R80ST (a pure street version of the R80G/S) and fully faired budget R80RT tourer, also introduced in 1982, likewise failed to sell. But BMW needn't have worried. In 1983, it finally released the first transformative K models with longitudinal four-cylinder in-line engine. This new generation of motorcycles would secure BMW's future for the coming decades.

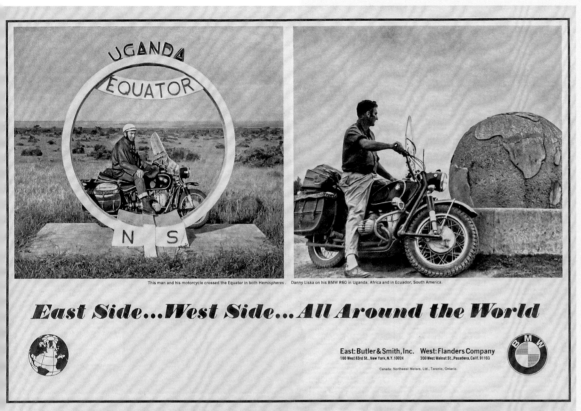

This man and his motorcycle crossed the Equator in both Hemispheres .   Danny Liska on his BMW R60 in Uganda, Africa and in Ecuador, South America.

East Side...West Side...All Around the World

East: Butler & Smith, Inc.   West: Flanders Company
160 West 83rd St., New York, N.Y. 10024   200 West Walnut St., Pasadena, Calif. 91103
Canada: Northwest Motors, Ltd., Toronto, Ontario.

• Adventure Tales

The Paris-Dakar Rally wins secured an immediate reputation for the R80G/S as the bike of choice for adventure-seeking travelers, especially as it came with an optional solo seat and long range 32-liter (8.5 gallon) fuel tank. In fact, it launched adventure touring as an entire new genre of motorcycle travel. Pretty soon, riders were making round-the-world (RTW) journeys and writing books about their experience.

Danny Liska of Nebraska had already set an example when in 1959–1961 he rode his R60 in two stages from the Arctic Circle in northern Alaska to Ushuaia, at the southernmost tip of South America; then in 1963–1964 rode from the north cape of Norway to the southernmost part of South Africa, resulting in a book: Two Wheels to Adventure (1989). And in 1982, 23-year-old Elspeth Beard set out from London on a solo motorcycle trip around the world on her R60/6. She shipped her already well-worn bike to New York and rode through North America before shipping it to Sydney. After a year working in Australia, she then rode her R60/6 home across Asia and Europe, becoming the first British woman to circumnavigate the globe on two wheels. Her travelog, Lone Rider, was published in 2017.

Also in 1982, Norwegian Helge Pedersen departed Scandinavia on his R80G/S, nicknamed "Olga," outfitted with a Heinrich 40-liter (10.6 gallon) fuel tank. He didn't return home for ten years, riding more than 400,000 kilometers (250,000 miles) through 77 countries on an epic RTW journey. (In 1988, he had taken 20 days to whack his way across the perilous Darién Gap, a 145-km-wide/90-mile swathe of roadless jungle separating Colombia from Panama.) He recounted his journey in 10 Years on 2 Wheels (1998).

Meanwhile, in 1985, Ed Culberson had tackled the Darién Gap (unsuccessfully) on his 1981 R80G/S "Amigo." Culberson persevered. The next year, he wrestled his Beemer through the swamps and jungle, and fulfilled his obsession of repeating Liska's America's-tip-to-toe journey while becoming the first person to cross the Gap with a motorcycle. In 1996, he published Obsessions Die Hard: Motorcycling the Pan American Highway's Jungle Gap.

Below left *Elspeth Beard was the first British woman to circle the globe by motorcycle.*

Below center *Sam Manicom and "Libby" (with spare tires and a 43-liter/11.4 gallon tank) in Botswana.*

Below right *Charley Boorman (left) and Ewan McGregor with one of their R1150GS Adventures.*

Investment banker Jim Rogers and his girlfriend, Tabitha Estabrook, chose a non-GS BMW R100RT and bikini-faired R80 to circle the globe in 1990. It took 22 months as they logged 105,000 kilometers (65,067 miles), resulting in the publication of Investment Biker (1994). English novice rider Sam Manicom tripled that distance on his rambling eight-year, 55-country RTW odyssey that began in 1992 aboard a R80GS nicknamed "Libby." In Into Africa (the first of four books regaling his journey), he writes: "As a novice motorcyclist, I carried far too many spare parts...My bike was so reliable that I hardly needed any of them." BMW management must have been pleased!

In 1995, an R80GS was journalist Patrick Symmes's choice to retrace Ernesto "Che" Guevara's revolutionary 1952 journey through South America on a 500cc Norton, as described in Guevara's classic The Motorcycle Diaries. Symmes narrates his own adventure in Chasing Che: A Motorcycle Journey in Search of the Guevara Legend. Meanwhile, having ridden a Triumph Tiger around the world on a four-year (1973–1977) odyssey—as portrayed in his best-selling literary travelog Jupiter's Travels—English journalist Ted Simon chose an R80GS to repeat his journey, setting out in 2001 (and detailed in Dreaming of Jupiter).

Thousands of adventure motorcyclists were now riding BMW GS models, although true RTW riders could still be counted in dozens. That changed in 2004 when motorcycle-mad actors Ewan McGregor and Charley Boorman set off from John O'Groats in Scotland on a 30,396-kilometer (18,887-mile) RTW journey by factory-modified BMW R1150GS Adventures. They were accompanied by a full television crew, including motorcycle-riding cameraman Claudio von Planta. The release in August 2004 of their blockbuster British television series Long Way Round (followed in 2005 by a best-selling book) turned motorcycle buying trends on their head. Every self-respecting motorcycle enthusiast was glued to the TV. The GS Adventures, which performed almost flawlessly throughout the trip, seemingly overnight became the world's most instantly recognizable and desirable motorcycle model. GS sales skyrocketed, while the adventure motorcycle segment became the fastest growing market, dominating all others.

R75/5

The launch of the /5 series in 1969 coincided with a shift in motorcycle market demand toward sporting performance. With its impressive 50-horsepower output and a top speed of 175 km/h (107 mph), the flagship R75/5—the first 750cc twin since the military R75 of 1941–1944—quickly established itself as BMW's top-selling model. Few, if any, bikes on the market could equal it for comfortable, high-speed, long-distance travel at the time. It handled well. It boasted classic BMW reliability. And it could cruise all day at 160 km/h (100 mph).

Though retaining its precursors' boxer layout, the all-new, much-improved engine borrowed several technical components from BMW's car engines, thanks to the designers drafted to BMW Motorrad from the automotive division. Among them, an automatic tensioning cam chain and stronger three-layer crankshaft main bearings. Gone were steel-cylinder barrels, replaced by aluminum-alloy barrels with a bonded cast-iron sleeve. New cylinder heads featured a much shallower 65-degree angle and larger openings for the valves. And the valve-actuation pushrods were now beneath the cylinders. Compared to its smaller R50/5 and R60/5 siblings, the R75/5 had a more radical cam profile, and a Bing Constant-Velocity (CV) carburetor provided a much smoother transition in power when the throttle was cranked open. An Eaton trochoidal oil pump to the rear of the cam provided high-pressure lubrication. A three-phase 180-watt alternator to the cam's fore powered the R75/5's new 12-volt electrical system. And magneto ignition with an automatic advance replaced the /6 series's battery-and-coil system.

It wasn't flawless, of course. Constant modifications were made, including to the ever-troublesome three-shaft gear-shift mechanism. And high-speed head-shake was an unnerving feature of the /5 series. In 1973, engineers stretched the wheelbase 50mm (1.97in) and extended the swingarm to cure the problem through better weight distribution: this also gave more legroom behind the engine, with footpegs now further back. Plus, a larger battery could be placed under the seat. The US market got restyled models for 1972, available in black, blue, or silver. Most notable was the chrome-paneled 17-liter (4.5 gallon) "toaster" tank and battery panels. It was derided and lasted only one year, when the chrome panels were replaced by rubber kneepads on a 24-liter (6.34 gallon) tank.

Above The year 1973 was a milestone for Bavarian Motor Works, which celebrated its 50th anniversary of motorcycle production, while this R75/5 was the company's 500,000th motorcycle to roll off the line.

The engine also got a new camshaft, centrifugal advance unit, and oil pump inner rotor. Nonetheless, the R75/5 was still behind the times in many regards. For one, it still had drum brakes. The Honda CB750 and Kawasaki March IV 750 had boasted disc brakes since they launched (like the R75/5) in 1969. Thankfully, the upgraded R75/6 got discs when introduced in 1973, along with a more powerful starter motor, new crankshaft, new closer ratio five-speed gearbox with new shifting forks, plus new turn signals and handlebar switches among the more functional and cosmetic considerations. And an optional touring package included a larger fuel tank and a windshield. However, the long spring travel of the front cartridge-type telescopic fork and rear twin shock swingarm combined with the righting moment of the shaft drive to cause unstable cornering on winding roads at high speed.

1969

R90S

By the early 1970s, the BMW board (and especially the vice president of sales, Bob Lutz) was beginning to despair at the growing competition from a new era of powerful Japanese bikes. To put the Japanese on the back foot, they needed to introduce something irresistibly novel. Not trusting the traditionalist nearsightedness of the motorcycle division, they assigned car interior stylist Hans Muth to the motorcycle design department. He set to work with passion and purpose to conjure a new flagship in the shaft-driven, boxer-twin model /6 series.

When revealed in 1973, the R90S caused a sensation. For half a century, BMWs had come in one color only—black as a Steinway piano. Not only was the R90S painted a jaw-dropping air-brushed metallic black-and-silver with gold trim (and in Daytona Orange in 1975), its contours could be described as nothing less than sexy. Key feature was a sublimely curved bikini cockpit fairing with integrated instruments. The bike virtually screamed "racy!"

The R90S received a tuned version of BMW's new 898cc R90/6 engine with higher compression (9.5:1) pistons, a stronger crankcase, and larger twin 38mm Dellorto carburetors nicknamed "pumpers" for their accelerator pump. Mated to a new, long-anticipated five-speed transmission, the R90S could run a quarter-mile (0.4km) in 13.1 seconds and go head-to-head at 200 km/h (124 mph) with a Honda CB750 in the straights.

Although relatively trouble-free, the R90S received BMW's obsessive attention to constant upgrades. In 1975, its penultimate year, the bike's troublesome transmission got new gear shifting forks, while new front fork dampers provided more compression and less travel. And the twin disc rotors were perforated to improve wet-weather braking (in 1976 they got larger piston brake calipers).

"Without question this is one of the top three motorcycles in the world," wrote *Cycle* magazine. "It has Superbike performance. Double disc brakes stop it in 130 feet [40m] from 60 miles per hour [97 km/h]. The engine is quiet and frugal, the cruising range is almost 300 miles [483km], and comfort at highway speeds is astonishing."

The comfort was due to a plush Denfeld saddle and twin Boge shock absorbers, new for the R90S. However, the soft suspension, extra-long travel and high steering inertia, and a new chassis with less rigid bolt-on rear subframe that caused frame flex combined to compromise the bike's sporting ability. But BMW had determined to produce an all-around performer acclaimed not just for its looks and performance but for its sheer versatility. That, and the R90S's heady $3,430 cost (almost twice as much as a Kawasaki 900cc Z1), guaranteed it celebrity status as an instantly collectable classic.

1973

B

technical
Sill 76

technical art

1976

W R100RS

ung: von 0 auf 100 km in 4,6 sec.
eschwindigkeit: über 200 km/h
DIN PS: 70 bei 7250 U/min.
Hubraum: 980 ccm

Opposite A 3-D cutaway of the R100RS showing the functional innards, from the front telescopic fork to the electronics beneath the fuel tank.

BMW's star stylist Hans Muth had wowed the motorcycle world with his R90S. In 1976, he conceived the equally ground-breaking R100RS. "I proposed to focus on the rider as a part of the motorcycle, of man and motorcycle as inseparable, like a modern centaur," recalled Muth of his visually arresting, fully faired Reisesport (sport tourer). BMW presented the R100RS at the International Motorcycle and Scooter Show in Cologne, alongside the bikini-faired R100S and unfaired R100/7—together the first-ever 1,000cc BMW models.

Other manufacturers had already used fairings, such as the Harley-Davidson Electra Glide's batwing and the Duo-Glide's big windscreen, engineered like a footballer to tackle the wind head-on. The R100RS was a whole new ballgame. A study in aerodynamic efficiency, Muth's elegant, fully integrated, injection-molded fiberglass fairing was optimized in Italian car designer Pininfarina's wind tunnel to slice through the air and provide downforce for increased grip and faster cornering. BMW claimed it reduced air resistance by 5.4 percent, and front wheel lift by 17.4 percent, contributing to the motorcycle's superb stability. As well as offering outstanding weather protection, it was also a true motorcycle cockpit with integrated dash featuring an ignition switch and analog instrumentation, including a clock.

The R100RS was powered by a more muscular version of the R90S engine, bored out to 980cc. The mill had new 94mm pistons, larger cylinder heads, and a compact reinforced crankshaft, with fuel fed by Bing 40mm constant vacuum carburetors, but the valvetrain was essentially that of the R90S.

It generated 70 horsepower at 7,250rpm, enough to power *the* bike to 200 km/h (124 mph) via the new /7 series's five-speed transmission.

Finished in a metallic silver blue, BMW's new flagship was the motorcycle industry's first modern performance-oriented sport-tourer. Its powerful boxer motor, strengthened frame (with thicker sections, a second transverse tube, and additional gusseting), and smooth suspension combined to guarantee superior high-speed handling through the twisties, even when fully laden.

Plus, you could cruise at 160 km/h (100 mph) all day long in comfort, while protected from the elements and in a relaxed sitting position (albeit a somewhat aggressive posture if using the optional solo sport seat) behind the fairing.

All this didn't come cheap. "Wallet-flattening," claimed *Cycle* of its $4,595 MSRP tag (twice the price of a naked, 1,000cc, flat-four Honda Gold Wing, introduced in 1974). But BMW had given the buying public a truly unique bike that for the first time combined the performance pedigree of an open-class sport-bike with the elemental protection of a luxury long-distance tourer. The R100RS was in a class by itself. There was no shortage of buyers.

R45

In 1973, BMW had discontinued the 498cc R50/5 and no longer had an entry-level vehicle in the popular small-capacity 500cc class. Between the end of 1973 through 1978, the 599cc R60/6 and R60/7 served as the smallest models available. Toward the end of the decade, BMW decided to again serve younger and first-time riders with medium purchasing power by launching the R45 as a little sister to the R65, to replace the R60/7 and compete with such mid-range Japanese bikes as the Honda CX500. Both were introduced in September 1978 at the International Motorcycle and Scooter Show in Cologne.

The new "small" (*kleine*) series R45 had a 473cc boxer twin engine with a 9.2:1 compression ratio and produced 35 horsepower at 7,250rpm. (A 27-horsepower, 8.2:1 compression version for the German market took advantage of favorable insurance rates for its class and became the best-selling motorcycle in Germany.)

1978

The engine architecture mirrored that of the larger boxers, but the short-stroke, oversquare 70mm x 61.5mm cylinders allowed smaller pistons and con rods, reducing engine width by 6.6cm (2.6in). A smaller diameter clutch and a lighter flywheel also saved space, while sharper contemporary styling by Hans Muth included an angular—and deceptively large—22-liter (5.8 gallon) fuel tank. Appearing compact and light, the scaled-down R45 had the personality of a perfect city bike.

The bike's all-new chassis with shorter front forks, lesser suspension travel, greater ground clearance, and 50mm (1.97in) shorter wheelbase (courtesy of a shorter bolted rear subframe) gave better handling than the larger siblings. But the R45's "smallness" was part allusion. With its dry weight of 205 kg (452 lbs) comparable to that of the 1,000cc twins, acceleration was anemic despite its being able to creep to a top speed of 154 km/h (95 mph). "Because of its lack of grunt, it had to be revved briskly in the gears to get it to accelerate," reported *Motorcycle Mechanics*. "You could find yourself swallowing your pride...as the engine repeatedly revs and dies in an awkward attempt to get away."

During the next three years, BMW upgraded the R45 (and R65) with a different final drive plus Nikasil cylinders, larger valves, and an additional crossover exhaust pipe to broaden the powerband and boost acceleration. However, the US versions retained a lower (8.2:1) compression ratio.

Being expensive, the competent yet underpowered R45 and R65 still didn't give much bang for the buck: in the US, at $3,445, the R45 was priced far higher than 1,000cc Japanese superbikes. Except for Germany, the smaller boxer never endeared itself with reviewers or buyers. During a seven-year run—1978–1985—a total of 28,158 were built.

R80G/S

Although now looking quaintly dwarf-like compared to today's BMW RI250GSA, when the R80G/S was released, it was the world's largest dual-purpose motorcycle. And its first! Visitors to the IFMA international motorcycle show in Cologne in autumn 1980 were agog at BMW's specialist new machine. Heretofore, no motorcycle had been produced that could tackle gravel paths and desert tracks and carry two people and their luggage in comfort on paved highways. The new all-rounder R80G/S boxer launched a new breed of "Reiseenduro" (touring enduro) machines.

Derived as a hybrid of the GS80 off-road racer and R80/7 tourer, it used the R65's twin-loop steel frame and a tweaked version of the R80/7's 798cc engine, with a lower compression ratio. Though considered heavy by off-road standards, it weighed 30 kg (66 lbs) less than the R80/7, despite the sump being protected by a thick, perforated, stainless steel bash plate. New lightweight, Nikasil-coated cylinders lopped 3.4 kg (7.5 lbs) off the bike's weight. The new clutch-flywheel combo saved another 4.7 kg (10.4 lbs) while improving the five-speed transmission's fluidity. And the R80G/S got a new smaller, lighter, maintenance-free Bosch electronic ignition system.

The leading-axle telescopic hydraulic front forks delivered a whopping 20cm (7.9in) of travel. At the rear, BMW introduced a revolutionary new right-side "Monolever" swingarm suspension system providing 17cm (6.6in) of travel. There was no axle, nor left-side swingarm or spring strut. Instead, the wheel hub was fixed to the rear drive crown wheel housing (as with a car), with a suspension strut on the right side and a shock absorber attached directly to the rear hub and main frame. The single-sided swingarm provided much greater torsional rigidity while being 2 kg (4.4 lbs) lighter than a traditional double-sided type.

Opposite *The R80G/S was the world's first true off-road-capable adventure tourer, capable of conquering even the Sahara Desert.*

Plus, there was nothing on the bike's left-hand side to obstruct the two-into-one exhaust system: it now ran up and *above* the wheel, which could now be removed in minutes by simply unscrewing three wheel-studs with the bike on the center stand. The Monolever rear suspension was prone to shaft-drive induced dip and rise. Nonetheless, the R80G/S boasted exceptional agility, steering, and handling.

For 1984, BMW celebrated the works team racers' Paris-Dakar Rally victories with a "Paris-Dakar" special featuring a huge 32-liter (8.45 gallon) fuel tank, protective bars for the cylinders, a single seat and rear luggage rack, and Michelin on/off-road tires.

The R80G/S was remodeled and upgraded in 1987 as the R80GS, while a 980cc engine producing 60hp at 6,500rpm powered a new R100GS version. These received innovative cross-spoke wheels, tubeless tires, and an innovative "paralever" rear swingarm with underneath torque support that improved handling in the same manner as a car's double-wishbone suspension. The paralever system is a patented feature of BMW motorcycles to this day.

R65LS

BMW had introduced the sporty-looking R65 in 1978 alongside the R45 as entry-level *kleine baureihe* (small series) models to compete with the innovative Japanese bikes that had swiftly come to dominate the small- and mid-size market. Hans Muth—the company's chief stylist—had turned BMW's formerly staid Teutonic twins into works of art with his smoke-faded R90S and spectacularly faired R100RS. In 1981, after leaving BMW to create his own design studio, he was hired to add a more radical look to the R65. The result was a new model: the R65LS, for "Luxus Sport," representing a racier, more refined version.

In 1980, Muth had designed the futuristic and streamlined Suzuki GSX1100 Katana. This stunner clearly inspired his R65LS, with its sporty, sharp-angled, wedge-shaped mini fairing and fastback rear end. Striking? For sure. A poster child? No! BMW traditionalists hated it.

The triangular fork-mounted cockpit fairing shrouded the headlight and an integrated, sloping black instrument nacelle (with an odometer, a tachometer with 7,500 redline, and—in the US—a government-mandated analog 85 mph [137 km/h] speedometer).

It was too small to add any wind protection. But BMW claimed that the fairing acted as a spoiler that reduced front-end lift by 30 percent. Truthfully, it was more an edgy styling feature than a functional fairing. Beneath the extreme styling veneer was a more-or-less stock R65 engine and chassis, with upgrades unique to the LS, including a curvier dual saddle, molded passenger handgrips in the tail section, a flat-black plasma-sprayed exhaust, unique color schemes selected by Muth, and more radical composite cast-alloy wheels (first seen on the 1976 R100RS).

The R65LS also got some performance upgrades. The front wheel's twin-disc brake with Brembo calipers enhanced stopping power, aided by the rear wheel's enlarged drum brake. And a stiffer front suspension improved handling through the twisties. In fact, powered by the R65's short-stroke 649.6cc engine (with horsepower upped to 50-horsepower for 1981), this sporty looking model with lower handlebars and a low center of gravity was praised as a responsive ride.

Although a capable sport tourer, its performance was identical to that of the standard R65. The overall finish wasn't up to BMW's usual standard. And Muth's Hennarot (flame red) color scheme with white-painted alloy wheels and black chrome features was considered garish. Plus, the R65LS seemed outrageously priced with a listed MSRP of $4,000 in the US ($400 more than the R65). Competitive Japanese motorcycles sold for half the price and had far more horsepower. The R65LS was discontinued in 1985.

1983

Die BMW Funduro.

2002

K-BIKES
AND THE RETURN
OF THE SINGLE

THE K-SERIES

European and US motorcycle manufacturers were caught flat-footed by the rapid emergence of Japanese bikes in the 1970s. With their amazing performance and reliability at affordable prices, these liquid-cooled four-cylinder machines were stealing market share by challenging BMW's claims to manufacture premium-priced superior bikes. British motorcycle marques tried to beat the Japanese at their own game but offered too little too late to save BSA and Norton Villiers Triumph from their demise.

BMW, however, was determined to maintain its reputation for building the world's finest motorcycles. The company was aware that its air-cooled, carb-fueled, "boringly reliable," horizontally opposed boxer engine was approaching its expiration date, especially in the face of ever-more stringent emissions regulations. The superiority of liquid-cooled, fuel-injected engines was a major selling point for Japanese manufacturers. To compete, BMW needed to introduce a clean-burning four-cylinder motorcycle quickly, and one true to the company's image. Instead of simply copying the Japanese model, it developed something totally unique— something that would continue to justify BMW's hefty price tag.

Revealed at the 1983 Paris Motorcycle Show, the new motorcycle was as different from the R series as imaginable. The venerable BMW boxer had seemed set in stone after 60 years in service. The new bike looked so unfamiliar, it caused a sensation. The bike was the K100, powered by a liquid-cooled, dual overhead cam (DOHC), four-cylinder, 987cc engine. BMW's first completely new engine design since the days of Max Friz was based on a prototype, initiated in 1977 by BMW engineers Josef Fritzenwenger and Stefan Pachernegg, using a liquid-cooled Peugeot 104 car engine placed longitudinally in a motorcycle chassis, instead of across the frame in Japanese fashion. They also tipped the engine on its side, with the crankshaft on the right and the cylinder head beside the rider's left foot, so that pistons moved horizontally (like the boxer engine).

The lateral layout lowered the bike's center of gravity (vastly enhancing its handling), while

the crankshaft's straight-line drive to the rear wheel allowed for use of BMW's traditional shaft drive. The K series also got the rear single-sided swingarm drive/suspension from the R80G/S. Its state-of-the-art Bosch LE Jetronic fuel-injection system (birthed in BMW's automotive division) was the motorcycle world's first.

Five years in development, the K100 launched as the basic R roadster sporting a small cockpit fairing, the fully clad RS sport tourer,

and the RT classic tourer. They all shared the same space-frame chassis, with the engine bolted on and suspended from it as a stressed member.

The K100 was a fantastic ride, with plenty of power and sporty, sure-footed handling. It was sophisticated, sharp-looking, and ultra-reliable. Still, many BMW purists complained that the company was betraying its heritage. An iconic new line had been birthed alongside the outdated boxer (which was about to be resuscitated as a more modern version).

Opposite *Design study for the aerodynamically sleek K100RS sport tourer, with an angular half-shell fairing.*
Above *The head of the BMW Motorrad design department is discussing the final version of the K100 with a designer.*

BMW K1

Meanwhile, in 1985, BMW introduced a counterbalanced three-cylinder variant of the K series—the 740cc K75—with the same bore and stroke but with higher (11.0:1) compression and a higher state of tune to boost power. The K series became best-sellers.

Despite annual updates, however, by 1988 the K100's 90 horsepower output was lagging far behind that of the competition. At that September's IFMA show in Cologne, BMW caused a stir with the über-radical K1. Designed to compete with the Kawasaki ZX-10, Triumph Daytona 1000, and similar rocket-ship sports bikes, the four-valve, 987cc machine relied on an eye-popping aerodynamic full-body fairing for high speed (many competitors boasted 140hp or more, but BMW voluntarily adhered to German regulations restricting motorcycles to 100hp). Its 0.34 drag coefficient was the lowest of any motorcycle made to date. But the controversial bodywork wasn't helped by its lurid ketchup-and-mustard paint job. At slow speed, the heat buildup inside the bodywork was acute.

Sectional cutaway of the controversial K1 showing the innards behind its radical and aerodynamic full-body fairing.

Plus, it was heavy. Albeit fast, performance fell short of the mark. Nonetheless, this two-wheeled technology showcase helped shift BMW's public persona from a maker of conservative tourers to a manufacturer of state-of-the-art, high-speed sports bikes.

All the technology that bulked up the bike—four-valve heads, electronic fuel injection, catalytic converter, and an anti-lock braking system—would soon make its way into the rest of BMW's model lineup.

BMW's newfound status was secured in 1996 with the release of the spectacular 130hp K1200RS. This gorgeous sport tourer with a light aluminum frame and BMW's patented Telelever front suspension performed as well as it looked. Meanwhile, after 11 years of service, the K75 series bowed out that year. But the annually updated RS and a fully dressed LT luxury tourer—the 1,092cc K1200LT—introduced in 1991 to take on the Honda Gold Wing are still steadfast sellers considered among the finest motorcycles in the world in their respective classes.

The faired, three-cylinder 740cc K75S proved an instant top-seller when introduced in 1985. It enjoyed a 10-year production lifespan.

BMW R 100 GS

FROM AIRHEAD TO OILHEAD

Although many BMW loyalists feared that the introduction of the K bikes would doom the boxer, the company realized that to discontinue the traditional layout would mean disowning an icon and an identity. Instead, it would build two engine types, with distinct models massaged to distinct market niches.

The G/S bike's success in the Paris-Dakar Rally greatly bolstered enthusiasm for the boxer, reflected in unexpectedly large sales for the R80G/S introduced in 1981. In 1984, BMW began a major redesign of the engine, experimenting with various cylinder, valve, and camshaft layouts, as well as rethinking the suspension and chassis. Having already ceased production of its R100 series, in 1987, the company bored out the 798cc R80G/S engine for a bump to 980cc, becoming the R100GS. The engine was then fitted to the resurrected R100RS and R100RT models, which also gained the G/S-proven Monolever rear suspension. The following year, BMW released a new commemorative model—the R100GS Paris-Dakar—closer in design to the real rally version. This showroom star (today a collector's item) set a template for the Adventure series that to this day remains the world's most accomplished and definitive enduro tourer. In 1998, the R100GS was the first BMW to be fitted with the company's new—and revolutionary—Paralever rear suspension.

By the close of the 1980s, BMW sales were more or less evenly split between the newer in-line K models and the traditional boxer bikes.

Above This technical 3D cutaway was used by BMW to promote the R100GS.

Opposite above The R100GS is considered a collector's classic in its much-covered special edition black-and-yellow "Bumblebee" colors.

Opposite below The first generation R100GS was the first BMW to feature the revolutionary Monolever rear suspension.

Finally, after years of development, in 1993, BMW unveiled its all-new and much-anticipated "oilhead" boxer. Completely redesigned, this new generation engine (code-named the R259) was a radical departure from its precursor. At 1,085cc, BMW's largest boxer twin to date combined air and circulated oil to cool its Nikasil-coated cylinders. The four-valve heads each had a chain-driven camshaft using pushrods and rocker arms to actuate the valves. And the 10.7:1 pistons were one-third lighter. To keep things cool, the R259 employed two oil pumps that circulated oil through internal galleries in the cylinder heads and then via an oil cooler and back to the sump. A second oil circuit was used for lubrication.

The R259 was introduced on the flagship R1100RS sport tourer, then on the R1100GS the following year. The bikes came with an all-new chassis, with the engine supporting front and rear subframes as a stressed member, as in the K bikes. And the well-established Paralever rear suspension was paired with an entirely new Telelever front suspension with Showa shock plus a V-shaped swingarm hinged off the engine cases.

The new generation boxer lineup gradually expanded during the next few years as the R100 models were replaced. By then, BMW had also introduced its first single-cylinder motorcycle in three decades.

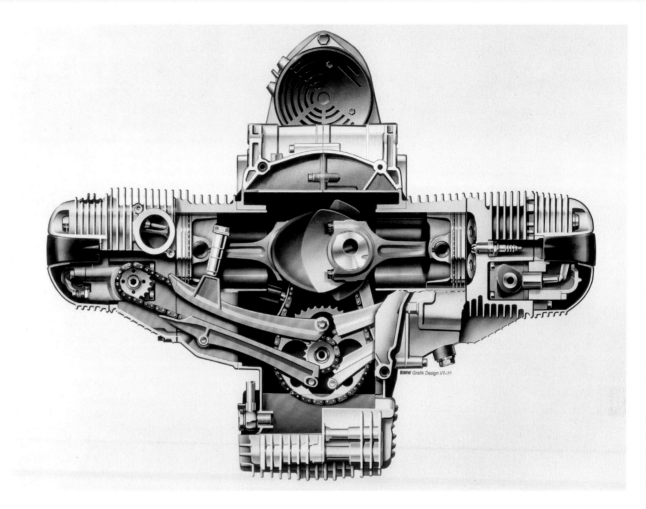

BMW F 650 GS

F 650 GS.
Für jeden Spaß zu haben.
Die BMW Funduro.

BMW F 650 GS

RETURN OF THE SINGLE (F SERIES)

As popular as the K and R series bikes proved, their increasingly large displacements edged them ever-further away from the entry-level market. BMW hadn't offered an affordable entry-level bike since retiring the single-cylinder R27 in 1966. The moment seemed right to make up for lost time. It did so in very un-BMW fashion.

In 1992, Italy's Aprilia began producing its 652cc Pegaso motorcycle using a five-valve, liquid-cooled, single-cylinder engine manufactured and shipped ready-made to the factory by Rotax of Austria. BMW executives figured a collaborative arrangement for their own branded four-valve version would be ideal. BMW engineers and freelance stylist Martin Longmore reconfigured the Pegaso concept to their desire (not least a styling resemblance to the R-series boxers), then outsourced manufacture to Rotax and Aprilia, with final assembly at the latter's Italian factory.

The bike launched in twin versions: the street-oriented F650St Strada and F650 Funduro dual-sport bike. The Funduro was slightly larger than the purely urban-focused Strada. The dual-sport variant had more ground clearance, a taller seat height, a higher fairing, a longer wheelbase, and a larger (48cm/19in) front wheel, all of which made it off-road capable in light terrain. Otherwise, the siblings shared the same liquid-cooled, DOHC engine, with 8.8:1 compression, and five-speed gearbox. Most noticeably, the F650 dispensed with a Cardan drive shaft. It was the first BMW motorcycle that used a roller chain to deliver power to the rear wheel. BMW traditionalists were once more aghast. But novice riders loved it, as did women motorcyclists.

BMW had hit pay dirt with an ideal entry-level model that, in 2000, morphed into the more off-road capable, two-cylinder F650GS, the most successful selling model in BMW's range.

Opposite The hugely successful F650GS came in a variety of lively colors, including "Mandarin" yellow.
Above Originally available only in red or yellow, the F650 Funduro was a sensible road bike, but with raised suspension travel was powerful and light enough for off-road adventures.

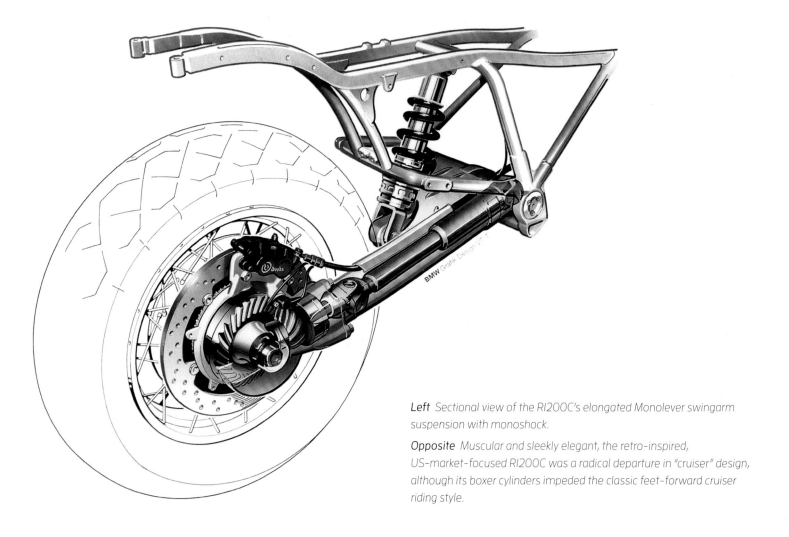

Left *Sectional view of the R1200C's elongated Monolever swingarm suspension with monoshock.*

Opposite *Muscular and sleekly elegant, the retro-inspired, US-market-focused R1200C was a radical departure in "cruiser" design, although its boxer cylinders impeded the classic feet-forward cruiser riding style.*

BMW BAGGER

As the millennium approached, BMW had its eye on another untapped market segment: the cruiser-obsessed US rider. "Cruisers" comprise more than half of all new bikes sold in the US, where the growly, torquey, low-slung Harley-Davidson "baggers" have long been king of the highways. The Honda Valkyrie, Kawasaki Vulcan 1500, and Yamaha V Star were already thundering down Route 66 in pursuit. Surely the Bavarians wouldn't compete!

In 1997, BMW shocked the motorcycling world with its stunning, heavily chromed R1200C Cruiser.

"Completely original, it will annoy the narrow-minded and expand the definition of a cruiser," opined *Cruiser* magazine. Here was proof that BMW was no longer the staid, conservative manufacturer of old. Although designed in Germany (albeit by American designer David Robb), it exuded a kind of "born in America" badass attitude with its sleek, long, low profile, high-rise handlebars, and exposed skeleton laden with chrome.

Its 1,170cc, 61hp, "oilhead" boxer engine was tuned very differently to the R1100's 88hp engine on which it was based. The latter had more power and torque, but the R1200C's torque was much lower down and still present all the way through a much lower redline. The bike's top speed of 168 km/h (104 mph) was perfectly adequate for serene cruising. It sounded throatier, true to cruiser tradition. And a low saddle and high bars offered a classic, relaxed riding position. But the boxer cylinders got in the way: the R1200C rider couldn't place his feet on traditional cruiser floorboards. At least the seat had a backrest, which could be folded down as a seat for a pillion passenger. A dual saddle was available as an option. And the R1200C could be customized with a range of distinct handlebars, panniers, screens, and other accessories.

The R1200C in various variants sold well through 2005, when the series was discontinued. By then, the same engine with same capacity and bore and stroke had been revamped and re-tuned to power the 2004 R1200GS and other models.

K100

When the new K generation of motorcycles was introduced in 1983, BMW was making a momentous leap. With its water-cooled, fuel-injected, longitudinal, four-cylinder in-line engine, the K100 was an entirely different Teutonic master machine whose shaft drive was the only recognizable BMW design element. Inspired by the need to meet stringent new US emissions standards, BMW engineers conjured up an uber-efficient, 987cc flat-four engine, flipped it on its side, then turned it 90 degrees and mounted it to a tubular space-frame chassis, with the motor as a stressed member. The entire powertrain (including gearbox plus integrated drive shaft with single swingarm) formed a single unit that BMW called the "Compact Drive System."

The eight-valve engine lay low and in line with the motorcycle frame: the cylinders, pistons, spark plugs, camshafts, and injectors were on the left side, and the crankshaft on the right. The K100 got a BMW automotive Bosch LE Jetronic ignition and fuel injection system with a Bosch fuel pump inside the 22-liter (5.8 gallon) aluminum tank, plus an under-seat computer to regulate intake-tract pressure, engine revs and temperature, and fuel delivery. The K100 claimed 90 horsepower and despite its low state of tune boasted an impressive top speed of 215 km/h (134 mph). Acceleration was brisk through a linear torque curve to the redline at 8,650rpm. The K100's low center of gravity and relatively short suspension travel guaranteed agile and sporty handling.

With its aerodynamic ground-hugging look, the unfaired "Flying Brick" (and cockpit-faired K100C) appealed to a previously untapped market. In 1983, BMW introduced the taller-geared K100RS sport tourer (capable of an extra 5 km/h [3 mph]) with angular, eye-catching half-shell fairing; it was crowned "Motorcycle of the Year" on four occasions. In 1984, the line was further expanded by the fully faired K100RT long-distance tourer with integrated side-panniers. And for 1986, the K100LT luxury tourer was added, with a higher screen and additional standard equipment.

All four K models shared the same engine platform with 10.2:1 compression and had dual front and single rear disk brakes. Later models got four-valve-per-cylinder heads, rubber-mounted engines, BMW's patented Paralever rear suspension, and the motorcycling world's first anti-lock brake (ABS) system. Meanwhile, the Jetronic fuel injection was replaced by a state-of-the-art Motronic engine management system.

The K100's success prompted the launch, in 1985, of a considerably slower, three-cylinder, 740cc K75 series, with Basic, C, and Sport versions. To boost engine power to 75 horsepower (only 68hp for the US), the K75 engine was given 11.0:1 compression, longer valve timing, redesigned cylinders, shorter intake manifold, and a retuned exhaust. A round headlamp replaced the K100's huge and ungainly square headlamp. The naked K75 proved to be the most successful K model and the top-selling BMW bike of its era.

Right The lateral layout of the K100's four-cylinder engine permitted a direct straight-line drive to the rear wheel from the crankshaft.

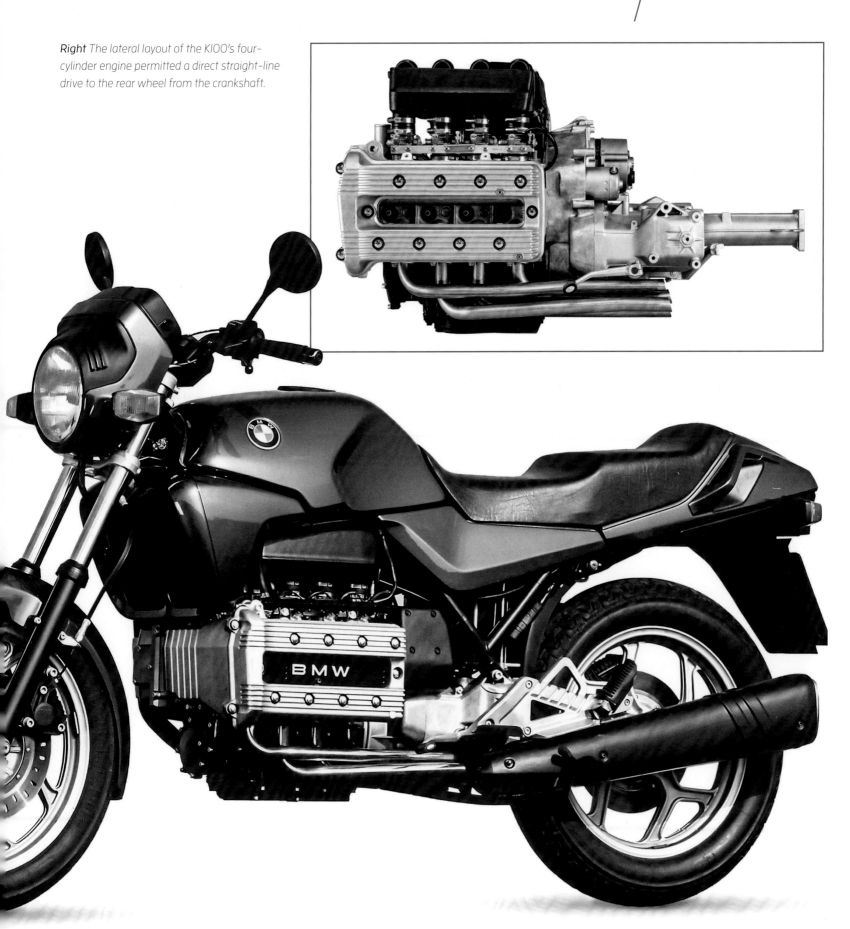

R80RT

The R80RT (for "touring") was introduced in 1982 as the first motorcycle (along with the BMW R100RS) to feature a full faring as a standard feature, and it had a two-year lifespan before a new Monolever swingarm rear suspension version was presented in 1984. The R80RT got more extensive cosmetic modifications (such as new bodywork contours, a more dynamic-looking front mudguard, and a new bench-seat) than the basic, unfaired R80 model, but it was relatively devoid of the excessive gadgetry of the competitive Japanese tourers.

The R80RT's generous streamlined tourer fairing with a high windshield offered exemplary protection against wind and rain. The fairing's two small adjustable vents to either side of the headlight, however, offered scant air-flow for hot-weather cooling. With its full fairing, it was unique as a relatively lightweight, mid-displacement alternative to the behemoth Harleys and Honda Gold Wing. Nonetheless, despite its aerodynamic efficiency, the fairing's large frontal area and the bike's relatively heavy weight-to-power ratio precluded it from becoming a stellar performer.

The R80RT was powered by the proven Type 247, 798cc, two-valve, OHV boxer engine built into the frame of the R100RT, but now fitted with electronic ignition, and new rocker-arm bearings for reduced valve-train noise. Putting out only 50 horsepower, with its five-speed transmission and lower final-drive gearing than the R100RT (the top two gears were too close to make the best use of the mill's wide powerband), it had moderate acceleration and a modest top speed of 170 km/h (106 mph). However, its excellent fuel economy and plentiful mid-range torque were perfect for long-distance touring.

Hailed as among BMW's definitive 1980's airheads, it was a near-perfect sport tourer. Many reviewers considered it the best-handling pure touring bike on the market. The R80RT/2 was much more responsive than the earlier model (and the heavier, twin-shock R100R) thanks to its exceptionally low center of gravity, 45.7cm (18in) aluminum cast front wheel, and gas-charged Monolever rear shock and swingarm with four spring-preload positions. It could be flicked through tight corners and twisties, and soaked up long winding country roads and any irregularities with aplomb.

The R80RT enjoyed a relatively long life—from 1982 to 1994—with a total of 29,384 made.

K1

By the late 1980s, BMW traditionalists were up in arms over their belief that the company seemed to be turning its back on its steadfastly Teutonic, time-honored touring twins in favor of some very un-BMW-like machines. The Bavarian firm appeared to be suffering an identity crisis. Then, at the 1988 Cologne Motor Show, it unveiled a radical "racer" the traditionalists considered grotesque. The bike was the four-cylinder, 1,000cc K1.

The controversial love-it-or-hate-it machine featured a gasp-inducing aerodynamically refined body that encompassed a huge, enveloping two-piece front mudguard, panniers built into streamlined side panels, and a high-rise enclosed pillion tail.

Plus, the garish ketchup-red paint job with bold mustard highlights spelling out "KI" was enough to make traditionalists vomit. More forward-thinking fanatics adored it.

As with other recent radical models, the KI was conceived as a sports-oriented tourer to compete with Japanese market leaders and appeal to younger riders. Opting to adhere to a 100-horsepower maximum for motorcycles sold in Germany, BMW turned to aerodynamics and automotive technology (such as a new four-valve cylinder head and an upgraded version of the KIOO's Bosch fuel injection) to boost performance to 95 horsepower—the most powerful BMW made to that time. Its 0.34 drag coefficient was less than any other motorcycle to date. With a top speed of more than 240 km/h (150 mph), it was the fastest 100-horsepower series motorcycle of its time.

Although based on the standard KIOO chassis and engine, the KI was a very different creature, with design features—such as ABS brakes and 16 valves—that would take competitors almost a decade to introduce.

Despite the KI's impressive top speed, the seven-piece fairing added weight. The bike was heavy: 234 kg (516 lbs) bare, but more than 270 kg (600 lbs) fully loaded. Acceleration suffered. Although weight was carried low and well-balanced, the KI wasn't sports-competitive. To reduce weight, BMW made the fairing panels too thin. They cracked easily. Plus, they retained engine heat, which was insufferable at low speeds. (BMW eventually installed an under-fairing heat blanket to aid heat dissipation, but it proved insufficient.)

Unlike that of the KIOO, the KI engine was mounted directly onto the frame, which boasted larger diameter tubing and a longer wheelbase for improved high-speed stability. The bike also got the revolutionary new Paralever rear suspension from the GS models, plus ABS brakes (first offered as an option on the KIOO) with four-piston Brembo calipers.

Priced in the US at a whopping $13,000, it cost two or three times that of competitive Japanese models. The motorcycle press acclaimed it. But the public wasn't so sure. Although the garish ketchup-red (or metallic blue) was replaced by a more sedate and saleable metallic black for 1982, sales remained dismal. Its limited three-year production lasted from late May 1989 to September 1993.

R100GS Paris-Dakar

Following the popularity of the R80GS and R100GS (both released in 1987) and the Paris-Dakar Rally victories, BMW introduced a conversion kit for both models, with "trans-Saharan"-style accoutrements to make them more akin to the hand-prepared rally versions. In 1984, BMW had honored the rally victories with a one-year-only "Paris-Dakar" commemorative special, reminiscent of the rally bikes. For 1989, there was a new factory GS series model—the R100GS Paris-Dakar—that more closely resembled the near crash-proof rally bikes that had won renown in the grueling African rally. This beast of a bike instantly became an icon, as well as a must-have among adventure-minded travelers as the world's definitive enduro tourer.

Most pronounced was its gargantuan 32-liter (8.7 gallon) high-impact plastic fuel tank (with built-in storage compartment) that merged into a frame-mounted plastic fairing with integrated headlight assembly and instrument cluster. Tank and assembly were enveloped by a wrap-around steel crash bar with steel-grill headlamp guard. Steel "roo-bars" also guarded the cylinders (and, from 1993, an oil-cooler affixed to the bars), while twin vented aluminum skid plates attached beneath the engine and to the center-stand protected the sump and gearbox when negotiating rocky off-road terrain. A sculpted plastic air-dam added extra front engine protection, while an oversize plastic extension added length to the high-mount front fender. The street-going rally clone also got a small sloping windshield, huge handguards plus heated handgrips, and a tachometer. A solo saddle was standard equipment, as were BMW factory hard bags, a burly rear luggage rack, and narrow Metzeler on-road/off-road tires. It was offered in two special white-and-red color schemes with "Paris-Dakar" decals.

Left The R100GS Paris-Dakar paid homage in both style and capability to the rally-winning machines that conquered the Sahara Desert.

The GS/Paris-Dakar employed the highly capable, air-cooled, two-valve-per-cylinder, 980cc flat-twin boxer engine of the more conventional RS and RT models, but geared lower. It was also tuned for low-end torque, rather than top-end horsepower. The bike's shaft-driven rear end exhibited a strong tendency to torque right from standing starts. But the Paralever suspension system with floating gearcase (with single shock mounted to the frame) cured the prior model's tendency to a "pogo" rise and dip when riders rolled on and off the gas. And the long travel of the soft-spring front forks gave one of the cushiest rides of any bike made.

Although large, heavy, and far from nimble, the bike handled powerfully and securely off-road, and was a fantastic long-distance tourer with a 570-kilometer-plus (350-mile) range.

Production of the R100GS Paris-Dakar lasted until 1996 (in 1994, the name was shortened to "PD" due to licensing issues with the rally organizers). Many BMW aficionados proclaim the R100GS/ PD as the finest all-round airhead boxer ever made. Today, it's a collector's classic.

1989
1990

K1100LT

1991

In 1991, BMW's four-cylinder, four-valve, 987cc K-series engine was increased to 1,092cc and unveiled mounted exclusively in the new and sporty, top-of-the-line K1100LT "luxury tourer." The all-new upgrade to the K1100LT was intended to level the playing field against Honda's dominant Gold Wing deluxe tourer and ST1100 sport tourer.

The engineers bored out the K100's 67mm x 70mm engine to 70.5mm, replaced its eight-valve head with the K1's 16-valve head, then installed new cams and an upgraded Motronic electronic engine-management system with three-way catalytic converter that reduced carbon monoxide, hydrocarbons, and nitrous oxide emissions. The K1100LT was the first bike in the US so equipped. The best laid-down K-motor yet, it produced 100 horsepower at 7,500rpm. The engineers also optimized the torque curve and rejigged the gear ratios for more relaxed top-end cruising. It pulled like a locomotive all the way to the 8.5K redline and was blazing fast, outpacing the Honda ST1100, running 0–60 mph (97 km/h) in 3.5 seconds and the quarter-mile at 110.15 mph (177 km/h) in 12.12 seconds. It could reach a top speed of 210 km/h (130 mph).

Although many riders complained of excessive vibration, the ride was otherwise smooth and comfortable, and the bike amazingly agile. *Cycle World* considered the K1100LT's anti-lock brakes with Brembo calipers the best of any production motorcycle in the US. BMW gave the LT a Marzocchi telescopic front fork and its patented Paralever swingarm with single, adjustable rear shock.

Naked, it resembled other K bikes. But dressed, the K1100LT was a thing of beauty, especially following an extensive 1992 revamp that repositioned the fairing and replaced the stationary windscreen with an optical-quality plexiglass version with electric-motor adjustment. Instruments were more attractively mounted and now included a radio-cassette unit. The handlebar spread was widened. A plusher seat was now hinged, opening to reveal the engine-management computer and a comprehensive toolkit. And luggage cases and topbox were more waterproof and enlarged to each take a full-face helmet.

The K1100LT also came in limited edition "Highline" and K1100LT SE "Special Edition" versions. The "base" model had a sobering MSRP of $14,290, for which buyers got what many considered the best K bike yet.

F650

BMW had ceased production of its last single—the R27—in 1966. But the market had radically changed. During the 1980s, light, nimble single-cylinder enduro motorcycles exploded in popularity, including as fun urban rides. BMW wanted in on the trend. In 1993, after a 27-year hiatus, it reentered the single-cylinder market with the 642cc Funduro—a dual-sport bike that was smaller, less intimidating, and cheaper than the hugely successful, large-boxer GS series. Slender, sporty, and straightforward in appearance, it had great ergonomics and was easy and huge fun to ride. It appealed to all sorts of riders, including first-timers and, notably, women.

Although BMW engineers configured the new chassis and engine, the F650 was inspired by Aprilia's Pegaso 650 with a mill manufactured by Bombardier-Rotax in Austria. Rotax built the Funduro engines; Aprilia assembled BMW's first-ever chain-driven bike. Rotax's revised, well-proven four-stroke engine was given a K-series-style four-valve combustion chamber with dual overhead camshafts, shim-type valve adjusters, bucket tappets, and dual spark plugs.

A pair of constant-vacuum Mikuni carburetors fed fuel; twin-port exhausts helped boost output. It generated 48 horsepower at 6500rpm. Weighing just 189 kg (416 lbs), the F650 had a top speed of 163 km/h (101 mph).

The engine was bolted directly to a square-section steel frame (which carried engine oil in its top tube) as a stressed-member. The front telescopic forks had a generous 17cm (6.69in) of travel; the rear got a single shock with hydraulic preload adjustment. It had Brembo single disc brakes front and rear.

A perfect all-rounder, the F650 was quick and responsive in city traffic, and equally at home off-road, where its light weight and long-travel suspension put it leagues ahead of its huge GS sibling. The F650ST sport model, introduced in 1996, was an even more impressive street performer. The Funduro even came with a lowering kit for shorter riders: a modified swingarm and shock stop actually dropped the bike's center of gravity

The low-priced, entry-level Beemer proved perfectly in tune with the times, selling twice as fast as expected. It was taken out of production in 2007, by which time it had evolved into a more off-road-capable machine that sired the current GS series of F family dual-sport bikes.

R1100GS

For two generations, BMW's big twin-valve, air-cooled airhead GS boxer had set a defining benchmark for dual-sport enduros. In 1994, a new generation model—the R1100GS—with the latest four-valve, 1,085cc engine raised the bar yet again. *Considerably!* Maintaining the perfect balance of off-road/touring ability, it was the largest capacity, most powerful, and fastest dual-sport on the market. It also notched up several firsts: first enduro with ABS, first with three-way catalytic converter, and first BMW GS with an air- and oil-cooled engine, as introduced in the 1992 R100RS. It was also visually striking with its high, huge, and weird "duck's beak" front fender (and optional yellow seat).

The GS engine got a milder powerband than the sportier RS, with milder cams, lower-compression pistons, and new valve-gear now operated via a single chain-driven camshaft. A more upswept two-into-one exhaust also helped trim top-end power (80hp at 6,750rpm) for stronger midrange torque. Down the straights, the R1100GS could squeeze past 188 km/h (117 mph), but the riding experience felt most comfortable with a top cruising speed around 140 km/h (87 mph), and especially so given its sit-up-and-beg riding position.

Carburetors were replaced by fuel injection via BMW's state-of-the-art Bosch Motronic engine-management system. This featured an optional catalytic converter (standard on US models) plus a fuel-shutoff function, activated when revs exceeded 2,000rpm during idling as a fuel-saving measure. System sensors monitored engine revs, throttle position, oxygen mixture, air and oil temperatures and pressures, and emission levels.

The GS boxers' eternal nemesis was its clunky transmission. This, despite receiving upgrades made to the prior year's R100RS drivetrain. On the plus side, its innovative Telelever front end now had 19cm (7.5in) of travel—almost twice that of the RS—plus integral anti-dive properties and an adjustable front shock with five preload settings. A single, centrally mounted shock absorber for the rear Paralever was given remote pre-load adjustment. Together, they provided formidable off-road capability. And the optional ABS anti-lock plumbing could be deactivated for off-road.

BMW fitted the new GS with specially designed, tubeless, dual-purpose Michelin radials. With its massive ground clearance and superb suspension, it maintained the series' reputation for solid off-road trail handling. However, with a 240 kg (549 lbs) wet-weight (4.5 kg/10 lbs heavier than the RS), the R1100GS was no easy-to-flick-around dirt-bike! But with sublime, sure-footed street performance, it came into its own on irregular roads or in rain. Then, no other bike could touch it. Add in the 24-liter (6.3 gallon) fuel tank and luggage package and it was unrivaled for long-distance adventure touring. In 1999, the R1100GS was superseded by the R1150GS.

1994

R1100RT

1995

In 1995, the R100 series was superseded by the R1100R, R1100GS, and R1100RS, followed swiftly thereafter by a stunning new flagship model—the aerodynamically sensual R1100RT broad-band tourer. The new-generation boxer siblings differed in chassis details and trim but shared near-identical eight-valve, 1,085cc engines with 99mm x 70.5mm bore and stroke and distinct levels of tune. The R1100RT shared the robust sport-oriented RS mill, with a compression ratio of 10.7:1 delivering 90 horsepower (up 30 ponies over the R100RS).

Unlike the angular severity of the K1100LT's fairing, the racy R1100RT was passionately curvaceous. Manufactured from recyclable plastic, its wind-tunnel-developed, full-cover five-piece fairing displayed BMW's wealth of expertise in aerodynamics. The stylists had ease of maintenance in mind, too. For example, the valve covers could be removed with the fairing in place. You simply removed the seat to access the air filter. And the oil-level sight glass was visible through the left panel. The R1100RT's built-in cockpit boasted more built-in instrumentation than a Boeing 747, with easy-to-read gauges, warning lights, a digital clock, and liquid-crystal display for fuel level, gear position, and oil temperature.

As BMW's top-of-the-line boxer, it had superb touring ergonomics plus all the trimmings, including the K1100LT's distortion-free windscreen that adjusted through 15.2cm (6.1in)—via a switch on the left handlebar— from low-and-raked to high-vertical. Standard equipment included heated grips, a height-adjustable seat, two 12-volt accessory outlets, lockable hard luggage, and AM/FM cassette radio with rather feeble dash-mounted speakers. It also came standard with ABS braking, plus a state-of-the-art fuel-injection system with a regulated three-way catalytic converter. And BMW's proven Telelever/Paralever front/rear suspension virtually eliminated drive-shaft-induced chassis jacking while also guaranteeing sublime handing.

The R1100RT combined superb performance and set a new benchmark for ride characteristics and comfort required for long-distance touring. With a top speed of 211 km/h (131 mph), it had blistering acceleration, noteworthy for a 255 kg (563 lbs) motorcycle with a 25.2-liter (6.6 gallon) gas tank.

Whereas the venerable R100RT had cost $10,290 (MSRP), at $15,990 the R1100RT was the most expensive Beemer ever. It set a new gold standard for touring and sold strongly through 2001, when it was supplanted by the R1150RT.

K1200RS

Opposite 3D drawing of the BMW's patented Telelever front suspension with Showa shock, and V-shaped swingarm hinged off the engine case.

BMW had since the 1980s applied Teutonic discipline and adhered to a voluntary restriction on producing motorcycles exceeding 100 horsepower in the German market. In 1996, however, the company blew through the ceiling with its 130-horsepower K1200RS. Powered by a 1,172cc revamped version of the K1100S's dual overhead cam, 1,092cc engine, this would be BMW's last in-line, 16-valve, four-cylinder "RS" sport tourer. Power was boosted by a higher 11.5:1 compression, a crankshaft with 5mm longer stroke, plus lighter pistons and valves, ram-air intake, and other fine-tuning. The K1200RS was by far BMW's most powerful bike ever built to date. It looked the part.

Its striped silver-and-blue paint job suggested "race me!" But the K1200RS was more a high-speed distance bike (and a superb one), *not* a pure sports bike. Despite a top speed of 245 km/h (150 mph) without luggage, it was still far too underpowered and heavy to take on the likes of Honda's 160hp BlackBird or a Yamaha YZF-R1. And its torque curve peaked down low (117Nm/86ft-lb at 6750rpm).

1996

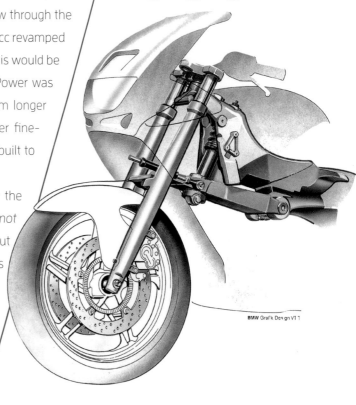

BMW Grafik Design VT T

But one twist of the throttle gave an addictive rush that made the most of the K1200RS's strong midrange torque and new high-rev power all the way up the tach dial. The refined sport tourer could go the long haul at rocket speed with passenger and luggage in comfort without breaking a sweat. Its 21-liter (5.6 gallon) fuel tank, however, was inadequate given the K1200RS's extreme thirst (16.6km/l or 39mpg), sufficient for a maximum range of around 320 km (200 miles) with a tailwind.

The ride was smooth, too, thanks to the new rubber-mounts for the engine (no longer a chassis stressed member) in a new aluminum-spine frame and to a new and far more responsive six-speed gearbox that was a revelation compared to BMW's traditional five-speed clunkers. The K1200RS featured adjustable handlebars, footrests, seat, and windshield, plus optional luggage. BMW even introduced optional cruise control.

The new chassis got BMW's patented Telelever front suspension and single-sided, single-shock rear Paralever, with the swingarm now pivoting on the frame. Twin floating discs with Brembo calipers (and optional ABS) provided state-of-the-art braking.

For model year 2001, the K1200RS was given a cosmetic facelift, and ABS was now standard. (A more powerful and heavier K1200GT version was introduced in 2003 and was produced through 2005, being replaced the following year by a totally revised transversely mounted four-in-line engine.) The sporty, head-turning K1200RS was discontinued in 2004 after 37,992 had been built at BMW's Spandau factory.

R1200C

Launched to fame—literally in a rooftop leap!—in the James Bond film *Tomorrow Never Dies*, the R1200C marked BMW's entry into the cruiser market in 1997. Although designed at BMW's Berlin HQ, and an eminently Teutonic BMW motorcycle, it was directly targeted at the US market and heavily influenced by classic Harley-Davidson styling to evoke freedom and the American Dream. Low-slung, with a scalloped solo saddle, raked forks, and high-and-wide pullback handlebars, this naked and muscular, retro-themed motorcycle had minimalist bodywork and was chromed to the max. It screamed to be ridden down Route 66 and California's Pacific Coast Highway.

The R1200C was powered by the R1100's four-valve opposed-twin boxer engine with fuel injection (with automatic choke and catalytic converter), and an increased bore and stroke for 1,170cc, but smaller valves for a third less peak power (just 61 horsepower) and lots of bottom-end torque befitting a cruiser. Although top speed was a modest 168 km/h (104 mph), it had heaps of low-rev power for overtaking in top gear without downshifting.

The motorcycle was built around the fully exposed engine as the chassis' primary structural member. The rear featured an elongated Monolever swingarm suspension that helped damp the classic BMW torque shift from the drive shaft during standing starts. The front featured BMW's radical new Telelever suspension with a separate spring/damper unit. A pair of large Brembo discs at the front and one at the rear provided immense braking power. ABS was an option on the base R1200C, which became known as the "Classic," offered in beige, black, or silver.

The R1200 was released in six variants, including a trike! For 1999, the Avantgarde model was a mildly restyled Classic with less chrome and lower handlebars. The millennial Independent (R1200C Phoenix in the US) saw other aesthetic changes, including a small windshield, fog lamps, and aluminum cast wheels instead of wire spoked wheels. In 2003, BMW introduced a full-dress bagger—the R1200CL "cruiser luxury"—with touring accessories, more instrumentation, revised front and rear suspension, and a lighter six-speed transmission from the more up-market K1200LT (a fancier CLC version even got a sound system). The resulting 20-percent increase in weight (to 308 kg/679 lbs) made the CL underpowered, especially compared to competitive baggers such as the Harley-Davidson Electra Glide. Finally, in 2004, a limited-edition Montauk was introduced, with fatter tires, an extended rake, and ABS as standard.

James Bond's spectacular rooftop leap in *Tomorrow Never Dies* perfectly depicted BMW Motorrad's daring and successful assault on the North American cruiser market. The R1200C had a run until 2005, with 40,218 "masculine and powerful" motorcycles sold.

1997

Above left *Sectional 3D diagram of the R1200C's four-valve, opposed-twin, 1,070cc engine with fuel injection and catalytic converter.*

Above right *Cutaway view of the R1200C's six-speed transmission first introduced on the K1200LT.*

R1150GS Adventure

By the millennium, BMW's GS and beefier GS Adventure were its consistently top-selling models. In 1999, the 1,130cc R1150GS with new six-speed gearbox replaced the five-speed, 1,085cc R1100GS, followed in 2001 by the heavy-duty R1150GS Adventure. The latter was the undisputed do-it-all motorcycle, a two-wheel Swiss Army knife perfect for sojourns in search of the ultimate off-the-grid-and-tarmac adventure.

As rugged and reliable as motorcycles get, the R1150GS Adventure was built for high mileage touring in arduous terrain. Armored up as an off-road warrior, it had taller front and rear suspension than the GS, offering 20cm (7.9in) of rough road–smoothing travel. It also got a 30-litre (7.9 gallon) fuel tank, a taller and wider windshield, lower gearing, dual front disc brakes, and an anti-knock sensor/adjustment that allowed the Adventure to run on low-octane fuel. Wrap-around engine guards, headlight protection, hand guards, auxiliary fog lights, plus metal side-panniers and rear top-case, were also standard on the Adventure. A solo seat, heated handgrips, and ABS brakes were options on both models, which left the factory with an aluminum bash-plate underneath as standard.

The Adventure's laced wheels came standard with all terrain tires. Albeit heavy, and noticeably more of an armful than the GS, when fitted with road tires the Adventure displayed superb long-distance ride-handling and comfort. Then, the lower gearing with seamless torque gave quicker throttle response around town and for highway touring. Nonetheless, while the huge fuel capacity gave greater range, it added weight and (together with the 5cm/2in greater ground clearance) raised the center of gravity enormously. Physically maneuvering the bike at slow speed was a handful.

Like the GS, it was powered by an air/oil-cooled, 85hp, boxer twin with electronic fuel injection and four valves per cylinder; in 2004, both GS models got dual spark plug heads, intended to reduce emissions and mid-throttle "surging." For 2002, the optional ABS system was replaced with an electronically servo-assisted combined rear/front ABS system.

With its mammoth fuel tank (and an average mileage, depending on conditions, up to 21 kilometers per liter [50 mpg]), the Adventure was unparalleled as a versatile, mile-crunching warrior. Sales of both models skyrocketed after Ewan McGregor's and Charley Boorman's 30,396-kilometer (18,887 mile) round-the-world journey, depicted in the blockbuster hit TV series *Long Way Round*. Some 58,023 R1150GS models (1999–2004) and 17,828 Adventure models (2001–2006) were made before being replaced by the more powerful and lighter R1200GS and R1200GS Adventure.

2002

2023

A NEW MILLENNIUM

BACK IN THE FAST LANE

For BMW Motorrad, the new millennium was reason to celebrate. Its financial troubles of recent decades were well and truly behind it. The new F series was a huge success, and the K bikes were proving equally popular. Both had opened up new market segments, while BMW's boxer twin models had never enjoyed so much success, thanks to the outstanding 1,170cc engine and the boom of adventure motorcycling led by the class-leading GS models. Meanwhile, the RS and RT bikes were selling like hotcakes to BMW loyalists and, in the RT's case, to police forces around the world. The company had even entered the "urban mobility" market with its enclosed (and short-lived) C1 scooter made by Bertone with 125cc and 176cc four-stroke engines manufactured by Rotax. With the dawning of a new century, BMW seemed determined to shed any lingering image of being boring in favor of a far racier persona. The next two decades witnessed rapid expansion as the Bavarian company explored new avenues, took new risks, and broke astonishing new ground in technology and high performance. BMW was back in the fast lane.

NEXT GENERATION K SERIES

BMW's engineers were busy developing a new F series parallel twin. The steadfast R series boxers were being redesigned. And the heavyweight (and comparatively overweight) K series in-line fours were being totally overhauled for the twenty-first century. The KI200 models, such as the 130hp KI200RS flagship "superbike" and KI200LT "supertourer," with their advanced technology, still used the laid-down engine placed longitudinally on a dated chassis. A more conventional transverse layout was in the works.

By the close of the 1990s, BMW Motorrad had decided to target the sport bike market by creating a high-performance machine that could compete with the best and, according to a company press release, "attain the same level of desirability and reputation that has always been enjoyed by BMW's M-division performance cars." In 2005, it unveiled the new KI200S, followed by R, R Sport, and GT variants, all with BMW's first across-the-frame four-cylinder engine. With huge low-down torque and top end power, the new K models were huge hits. That year also saw the advent of optional electronic suspension adjustment (ESA); a first on series production motorcycles, it allowed a rider to adjust suspension settings at the push of a button.

For 2008, engine capacity was bumped to 1,293cc, with output ranging from 160hp for the GT to a whopping 175hp for the S. The K bikes also got more cutting-edge electronic riding aids, including automatic stability control (ASC) to prevent the rear wheel from spinning out of control, HP Gearshift Assistant clutchless quickshifter, and BMW's anti-lock brake system (ABS) as standard. And Dynamic Traction Control (DTC) followed for 2009—another series production motorcycle first.

By the close of the decade, the KI300 series led the motorcycle world in state-of-the-art technology. Even better was to come with the launch of the KI600 series in 2010.

Introduced in 2005 as BMW's new sporting flagship, the KI200S featured groundbreaking technology developed in BMW's Formula I race cars.

Above A K1200S being fitted with BMW's new patented front Duolever suspension in the Berlin assembly plant.

Below The 2005 K1200R (and its RS, S, and GT siblings) were powered by BMW's all-new liquid-cooled, DOHC, 1,157cc in-line-four engine aligned transversely rather than longitudinally.

BOXER EVOLUTION

BMW's evergreen and astoundingly robust boxer twins spanned the millennium's motorcycling spectrum, from sports riding with the R1150S to globe-spanning expeditions with the R1150GS Adventure. But BMW one-upped itself by producing an astonishingly better all-new boxer motor for 2004. Launched that year with the R1200GS, the 1,170cc engine was an upgraded, more compact version of that used in the R1200C custom cruiser,

but now giving out 100 ponies (up from 85hp). The R gained a sixth gear. The rear Paralever shaft drive now had the torque arm above the shaft. And the entire chassis was reworked. BMW pared an astounding 30 kg (66 lbs) off the GS, making it faster and far more agile.

The full boxer range had been given the powerful new 1200 motor by 2007. It also found its way into an entirely new (and ultra-expensive) "High Performance" family—the purposefully aggressive, limited-production HP line. It launched in 2005 with the HP2 enduro (the "2" signifying two cylinders) in a Dakar-inspired chassis optimized for dedicated off-roading. The radical HP2 was followed in 2007 by the more powerfully tuned SOHC HP2 Megamoto road bike and, in 2008, by the boundary-pushing 130hp HP2 Sport featuring BMW's first double overhead cam boxer motor—its most powerful incarnation yet produced. By 2010, the DOHC had arrived in the GS, too. The three HP2 models were short-lived, however, ending production in 2012.

The HP2 wasn't the only revolutionary entry into the off-road market. In 2008, BMW reintroduced the F650 single, rebranded as the more enduro-focused G650X series, with a Chinese-made liquid-cooled engine. It didn't sell well. For 2007, BMW also launched a track-ready enduro scrambler—the G450X—with an all-new 449cc engine featuring some very left-field technology. When that year BMW also bought the Swedish Husqvarna Motorcycles, it seemed that riders would soon see a new range of BMW/Husqvarna models. It was ill-timed. The financial crash of 2008 hit the motorcycle world hard, and BMW sold Husqvarna to KTM in 2013.

Powered by a retuned 1,170cc boxer engine, the minimalist and lightweight, 105hp HP2 was BMW's first dedicated enduro motorcycle.

F SERIES REDUX

With its recent focus on new top-of-the-market K and R series engines and heavyweight motorcycles, BMW's middleweight models were now looking thin on the ground. Rather than reprise the milquetoast R850 models, it again partnered with Austria's Bombardier Rotax and developed a totally new and compact, cutting-edge, water-cooled, eight-valve, DOHC, 798cc engine. Unveiled in 2006 to power the F800S and ST models, it was BMW Motorrad's first new engine layout in decades. Since the twin pistons moved up and down together, engineers gave the parallel twin a long "nodding" balancer beam that, pivoting from the rear of the crank, traveled up and down in the opposite direction to the pistons to eliminate inherent vibration.

The motor had great economy, plentiful torque for touring, and powerful performance, best demonstrated in the F800GS adventure tourer (introduced in 2008) and F800R naked sport roadster (2009).

By now, BMW's pioneering work with ABS, electronic suspension, gearbox quickshifters, LCD dashboards, traction control, and trip computers—offered as options, or standard, on an increasingly large range of bikes—was miles ahead of Japanese competitors. The Far East had become a little complacent. Worse, the financial crash of 2008 severely impacted Japanese manufacturers due to a massive increase in the yen's value. Suddenly Japanese bikes were more expensive to buy in Europe and North America than BMWs! At least, Japan still had the superbike market sewn up. But that was about to change.

Seven decades had passed since BMW had produced a race machine that could keep pace with the competition. In 2009, it introduced the ultra-high-tech, chain-driven S1000RR superbike. Powered by a newly designed and "conventional" transverse-mounted, 999cc, four-cylinder in-line engine churning out 193 horsepower, it soon dominated superbike racing. In 2014, an S1000RR ridden by Michael Dunlop swept the big-bike board at the Isle of Man, including the Senior TT, 70 years after George Meier's historic Senior TT win. Buyers loved it! BMW had successfully tapped a whole new market and secured its image as a producer of the world's best motorcycles across the board.

Inevitably, BMW spun off the S1000RR into variants: for 2014, the naked S1000R roadster, retuned to produce "just" 160hp, and the equally powered S1000XR dual-sport with longer-travel suspension and vaguely GS-inspired styling. It also repackaged the S1000RR as the HP4 (2012) with an even more cutting-edge chassis and electronics, and the more extreme non-street-legal and non-race-legal HP4 Race (2017) for well-heeled track-day speed freaks.

"Unstoppable S1000RR" screams this BMW poster of its race-winning superbike powered by a groundbreaking, transverse-mounted, four-cylinder, 999cc engine.

THE LAST DECADE

BMW had sunk enormous money and time into developing the S1000RR. But the R&D engineers had also been at work on an all-new—in fact, revolutionary—six-cylinder in-line engine to replace the dated 1,200cc motor for its flagship K tourer series. The transversely mounted, 24-valve, DOHC, 1,649cc powerplant debuted in 2010 with the totally redesigned K1600GT and GTL. Although producing a modest 160 horsepower, its huge 175Nm (129lb-ft) of torque was ideal for powering the enormous 348 kg (767 lbs) curb weight of the K ultra-tourers. Reviewers were unanimous: the Honda GL1800 Gold Wing had finally met its match with the sleek, sportier, and more luxurious GTL.

Meanwhile, by 2012, the oil-cooled R1200GS and GS Adventure had enjoyed a decade-long run. They'd received constant updates, of course, including DOHC heads for 2009. Stylistically, they still looked dynamic. And they still sold well. But Ducati, KTM, Triumph, and others had been playing catch-up. New Euro4 emissions regulations forced the issue. For 2013, the R1200GS was entirely revised, now water-cooled and with a radical vertical intake/exhaust layout alongside the latest high-tech electronics, which were now controlled through a revolutionary, patented thumbwheel Multi-Controller on the left handgrip. By 2014, the R, RS, and RT models had also received the new motor.

The parallel twin F model range, however, had by now become muddled: there were now two 789cc GS models, with the confusingly named F650GS added for 2008 alongside the F800GS, but replaced in 2012 by the F700GS (also with a 789cc engine). The less popular S and ST sport tourers were replaced by the F800GT. For 2016, the series got upgraded, including with electronic "ride-by-wire" throttle control and pre-programmable rider modes for "Rain," "Road," and "Enduro" conditions. A major revamp of the entire F range for 2018 included new F750GS and F850GS models—both with an all-new 853cc engine, with different states of tune. That engine was tweaked again in 2019, producing more power for the new F900R and F900XR roadsters, with styling cues from the S1000RR.

Opposite The water-cooled R1200GS (introduced in 2013) featured the latest high-tech electronics and was considered the world's premier all-rounder bike.

Above The revolutionary Multi-Controller thumbwheel on the left handgrip allowed a rider to control the chassis and BMS-X engine management system, audio and navigation systems, and even the seat height and temperature without taking his or her eyes off the road.

IDEATION

The G650 single was ended in 2016, replaced in 2015 by a new entry-level, small-capacity, lightweight single—the G310R roadster. BMW's smallest-ever production motorcycle was built in partnership with India's TVS Motor Company and powered by a 313cc engine. A dirt-friendly GS model, added for 2017, resembled a miniature clone of the big R1200GS. BMW now had GS models in four distinct capacities. In 2019, the two big GS models finally received a totally new air-/liquid-cooled, 136-horsepower, 1,254cc boxer engine featuring the ShiftCam technology first introduced on the S1000RR. Its far smoother and punchier power delivery guaranteed a much more exhilarating ride. Plus, the R bikes now had all BMW's latest electronic safety features for enhanced control and comfort.

For 2012, BMW had even reentered the scooter market with the parallel twin, 647cc, high-performance C600 Sport and C650GT, followed in 2017 by the C400X and C400GT 350cc singles. It now seemed that BMW Motorrad had tapped almost every market segment. The company was approaching 100 years old, and since retro-themed heritage bikes were exploding in popularity, it was time for BMW to tap the nostalgia market. In 2014, it therefore reprised its venerable (yet duly high-tech-updated) 1,170cc oilhead boxer engine to power the all-new R nineT—a gorgeous contemporary homage to the iconic R90 of 1973. Its pared-down, back-to-basics design, including removable rear subframe, was purpose-built for customization from a menu of factory-made options. It was such a hit that several themed variations soon followed.

Above Concept drawings for the C650GT scooter.

Right Introduced in 2012, the C600 Sport scooter was powered by a 647cc parallel twin.

CENTENARY MODELS

For 2020, BMW went bigger yet with an entirely new air-cooled, OHV 1,802cc engine—the company's largest motor ever—fitted to a stunning new retro-themed big-bore cruiser: the R18. A superb harmony of heritage styling (this time inspired by the 1930s-era R5) and the latest high-tech, it exuded a panache that Harley-Davidson could only dream of. The following year, BMW added a Classic model with Harley-style saddlebags and windshield, the R18B bagger with a yesteryear-style BMW fairing, and the fully loaded Transcontinental heavy tourer. Weighing 427 kg (942 lbs) fully fueled, the sleek Transcontinental was BMW's biggest bike ever produced, and it outclassed even the Indian Roadmaster as the ultimate in luxurious travel.

In 2023, BMW Motorrad celebrated its 100th anniversary with chrome-lavished, all-black R nineT 100 Years and R 18 100 Years limited-edition specials. Only 1,923 of each were produced. Plus, the company had marked the 50th anniversary of BMW Motorsport GmbH in 2022 with a 50 Years M special edition of the M1000RR, introduced in 2020 as an even more powerful road legal variant of the S1000RR. The company sold almost 23,500 of the two scorchingly fast superbikes in 2022.

Opposite The R18 100 Years (left) and R nineT 100 Years (right) celebrate 100 years of BMW motorcycle production since introduction of the R32 (center) in 1923.

Right The limited-edition R18 100 Years boasts a two-toned black-and-oxblood-red solo seat with a stitched diamond pattern (above). Perforated exhaust tips in the form of the BMW logo decorate the R18 100 Years' Akrapovič mufflers (below).

That year, it also introduced its first all-electric bike, the CE04 commuter scooter, styled as if for a sci-fi movie. The electrified future had arrived as Markus Schramm, head of BMW Motorrad, announced that by 2025, other model series would be powered by batteries derived from BMW's i series electric cars.

In 2022, BMW Motorrad achieved the highest sales in its corporate history, topping 200,000 two-wheelers for the first time. For 2023, its centenary year looked golden.

Above *The zero-emissions, fully-electric, 42hp CE04 silent scooter, introduced in 2022, launched a new era in futuristic BMW design.*
Opposite *The avant-garde concept design for the minimalist CE04 urban commuter included a floating seat.*

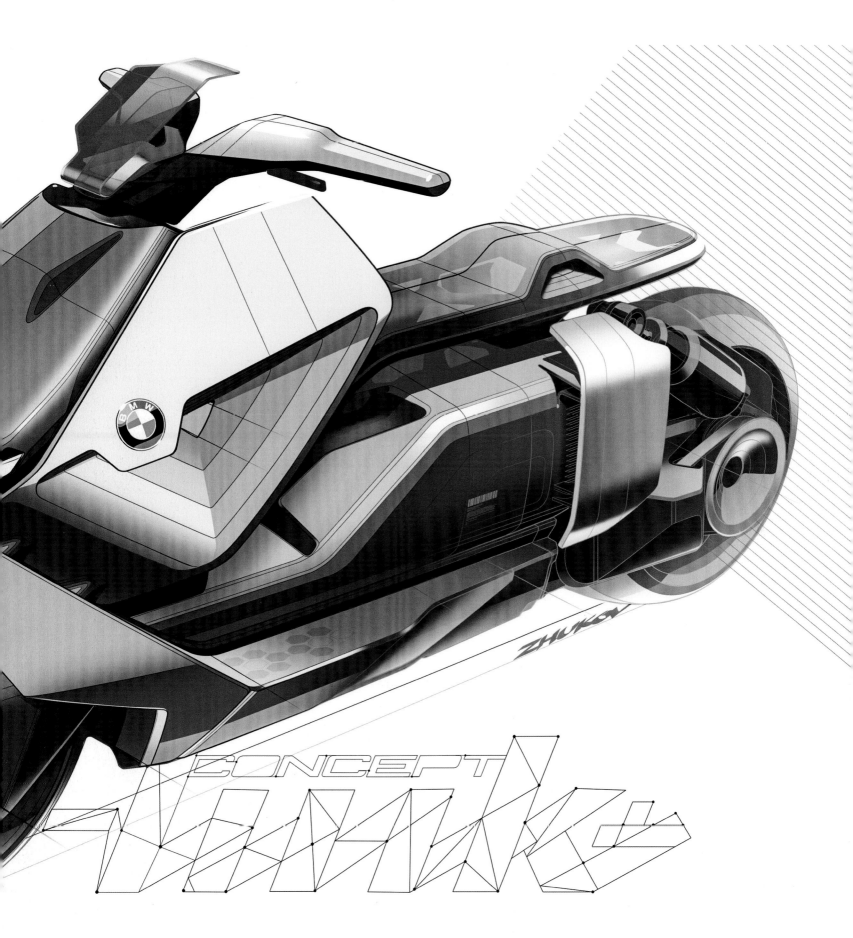

CONCEPT

ZHUKOV

Above Imagining a future decades from now, BMW designers created the Vision Next 100 BMW concept motorcycle, which morphs form and utilizes artificial intelligence.

Opposite BMW's next generation motorcycles will resemble the Concept 9cento superlight, carbon-fiber, 3D-printed all-in-one fusion adventure sport tourer.

• Vision for the Future

VISION NEXT 100

In November 2016, BMW revealed its vision for an exciting, decades-forward futuristic two-wheeler based on technology that currently can only be imagined for a digitized world in which vehicles function autonomously. Inspired by the classic opposed-twin boxer design and the R32's jet-black triangular frame, the minimalistic Vision Next 100 motorcycle features an elastic carbon-fabric Flexframe that morphs shape with steering maneuvers. The flexible frame, and self-damping tires that similarly adapt to changing terrain, eliminate the need for suspension or steering fork. The emission-free, polished aluminum engine has jugs that extend and retract like a bellows for optimized aerodynamics. Self-balancing gyroscopes ensure that no stand is needed; the bike stays upright when static. Nor does the rider need a helmet, thanks to the safety system's artificial intelligence: a glasses-like three-dimensional, augmented-reality visor provides "head-up" data display, as in an aircraft cockpit. (Much like a self-driving Tesla, the motorcycle corrects itself if the rider fails to react.) Pushing the boundaries of technology and styling, BMW's Vision Next 100 presents an image of motorcycling for the next century.

CONCEPT 9CENTO

A perfect amalgam of form and function, BMW's Concept 9cento—unveiled at the 2018 Concorso d'Eleganza Villa d'Este in Italy—revealed the company's vision for its holistic next generation of motorcycles. An agile, aggressive, sleek, and super-light fusion of compact sport bike and tourer, with a touch of light adventurer thrown in, it converts from solo sport bike to two-up tourer in seconds. This thanks to radical clip-on dual panniers secured by electromagnets that also function as a stylistically integrated rear pillion. Echoing the S1000RR crossover concept, the raised, narrow front section with long-travel suspension and swept sharp-angled fairing weds characteristics of BMW's sport and adventure sport bikes. The 3D-printed fairing and frame are carbon fiber reinforced polymer, as with the S1000RR. So is the swingarm, as in the HP4 Race. The Concept 9cento is to be powered by a retuned version of the BMW 853cc parallel-twin motor. Although no production date has been set, it looks like a perfect next-generation F850GS.

R1200GS

The immense success of BMW's class-defining GS multiplied with each new generation. In 2004, the R1200GS took it to a new level. What had begun in 1979 as a relatively simple large-capacity dual-purpose bike had morphed with the R1150GS into a hugely capable, yet somewhat top-heavy and cumbersome behemoth. With the fourth-generation R1200GS, it became a simply brilliant multi-purpose sport tourer. This because BMW had carved a remarkable 30 kg (66 lbs) off its weight, while also lowering its center of gravity, and because it introduced BMW's new 1,170cc boxer engine and a slew of innovative technological enhancements. The result: a GS that was truly exciting to ride.

Pumping out 100 horsepower (up 18hp) at 7,250rpm, the air/oil-cooled DOHC boxer motor got a 101mm x 73mm bore and stroke, larger and lighter pistons, a lighter crankshaft, and larger valves (now filled with sodium to aid cooling) inside reshaped hexagonal cylinder heads. The punchy engine churned out consistently smooth power and sharp acceleration throughout its range. It was vibration free, too, thanks to a new-for-BMW counterbalance shaft. The new six-speed gearbox had close-ratio helical-cut gears, with the top gear no longer merely an overdrive. And the electronic fuel injection was wed to a ride-by-wire throttle system. The GS's impressive increase in engine performance delivered a top speed of 210 km/h (131 mph)—remarkable for an adventure tourer.

The bike was equally dynamic and agile on pavement and dirt. The GS had finally become flawlessly flickable, whether tearing through twisties or flying over rocks and gravel. Credit the weight loss, a stiffened trellis frame, and a forged aluminum Telelever front suspension plus lighter Paralever shaft drive/swingarm suspension (now offering more ground clearance and sealed for life) with adjustable shock that together soaked up hits and holes without blinking. BMW's EVO servo-assisted brake system came standard, while optional ABS could be deactivated for riding off-road. And the R1200GS introduced such wizardry as "Rain" and "Road" ride modes, which adapted acceleration and traction control to riding circumstances.

2004

In 2008, the GS also got BMW's Electronic Suspension Adjustment (ESA), with sensors mounted on front and rear wheels adjusting the damping in response to changing road conditions.

For 2004, sleek shark-face side tank covers created a more aerodynamic look, aided by sharp-looking cast-alloy wheels. A height- and angle-adjustable seat and five-way adjustable windscreen came standard. And an owner could go broke purchasing heated grips, crash bars, luggage cases, and various other add-ons.

Practical, comfortable, rugged, and fast, the R1200GS could justifiably claim to be the world's most versatile motorcycle—a sophisticated dirt bike, sport bike, and touring bike wrapped into one. No wonder it enjoyed a nine-year run until 2012.

K1200S

Right Cutting-edge technology—from clutchless gearshift assist and dynamic traction control to touch-button electronic suspension adjustment—enhanced the blazing performance of the K1200S, BMW's most powerful motorcycle to date.

BMW's precipitous unveiling of the new K series's sporting flagship in the fall of 2004 was a public relations disaster: the bike was plagued by fuel injection problems and other issues that delayed the public release by almost a year. With the issues resolved, the K1200S hit the market in 2005 as the sportiest and most powerful BMW motorbike ever. A synthesis of all BMW had learned from decades of motorsport success, the bike's ground-breaking technology was purposed to define "maximum performance."

The all-new liquid-cooled, DOHC, four-valve-per-cylinder, 1,157cc in-line-four engine was the first K-model motor to be aligned transversely rather than longitudinally. Designed for compactness, low weight, and class-leading power, it was also angled 55 degrees forward to lower the center of gravity and optimize the bike's center of mass for enhanced traction and handling. Rated at 167 horsepower, the K1200S had breathtaking acceleration and a top speed of around 275 km/h (170 mph).

Tapping technology developed in BMW's Formula 1 race cars, the engine used flat cylinder heads, an ruber-efficient fast-burning chamber, and a very narrow valve angle with high 13.0:1 compression.

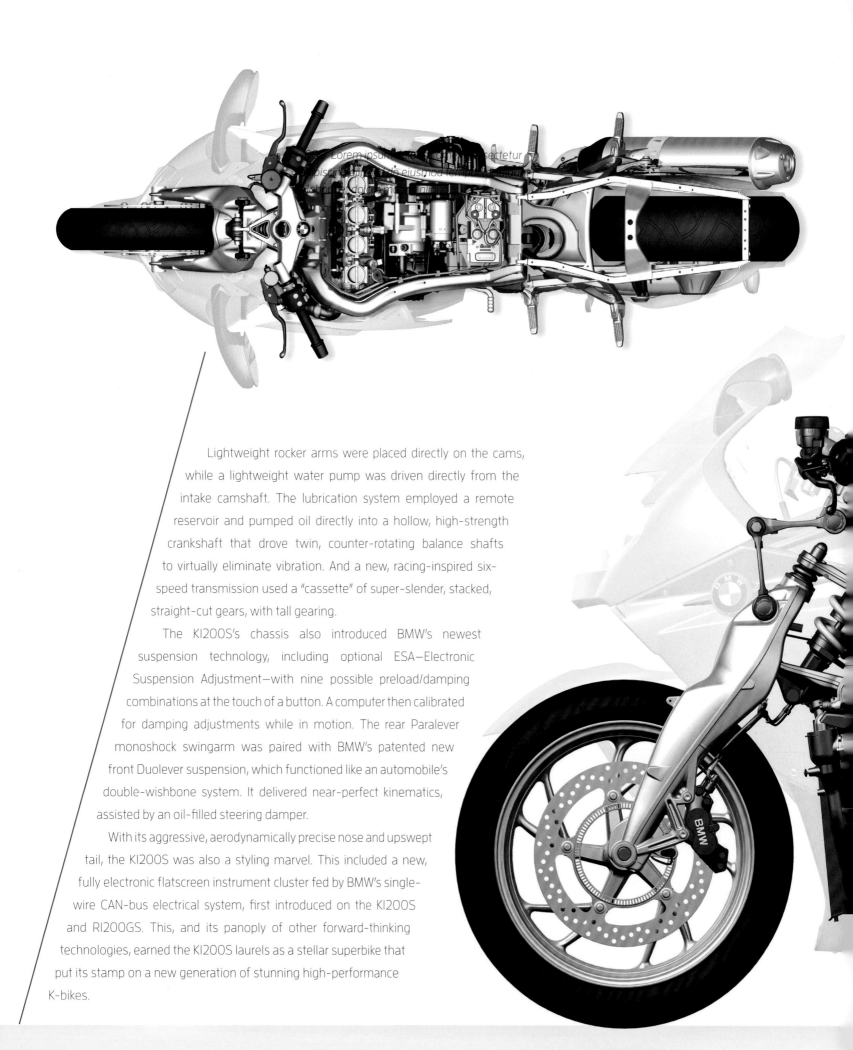

Lightweight rocker arms were placed directly on the cams, while a lightweight water pump was driven directly from the intake camshaft. The lubrication system employed a remote reservoir and pumped oil directly into a hollow, high-strength crankshaft that drove twin, counter-rotating balance shafts to virtually eliminate vibration. And a new, racing-inspired six-speed transmission used a "cassette" of super-slender, stacked, straight-cut gears, with tall gearing.

The K1200S's chassis also introduced BMW's newest suspension technology, including optional ESA—Electronic Suspension Adjustment—with nine possible preload/damping combinations at the touch of a button. A computer then calibrated for damping adjustments while in motion. The rear Paralever monoshock swingarm was paired with BMW's patented new front Duolever suspension, which functioned like an automobile's double-wishbone system. It delivered near-perfect kinematics, assisted by an oil-filled steering damper.

With its aggressive, aerodynamically precise nose and upswept tail, the K1200S was also a styling marvel. This included a new, fully electronic flatscreen instrument cluster fed by BMW's single-wire CAN-bus electrical system, first introduced on the K1200S and R1200GS. This, and its panoply of other forward-thinking technologies, earned the K1200S laurels as a stellar superbike that put its stamp on a new generation of stunning high-performance K-bikes.

Opposite *Cutaway detail of the KI200S's cast-aluminum skeleton chassis with pencil-thin tubular-steel rear frame.*
Below *The KI200S's sublime handling was enhanced by the 55-degree forward tilt of its in-line-four engine, BMW's rear Paralever monoshock swingarm, and the new Duolever front suspension.*

K1200LT

2004

BMW had launched its first luxury tourer in 1991 with the K100LT. In 1998, it was replaced with the completely redesigned—and visually and technologically more robust—K1200LT, equipped with integrated panniers, a stereo AM/FM radio, and BMW's own optional satellite-navigation system. But it was the beautiful, newly updated 2004 model that set the benchmark as the bagger market's definitive fully loaded luxury tourer. Far cheaper than a Honda Gold Wing, it offered more creature comforts and technological enchantments. It was also sleekly stylish and much sportier than the behemoth Honda.

The 2004 model had all the first generation's features (from a massive top-box to a height-adjustable windscreen). But it now came with such luxury enhancements as sumptuous heated seats, height-adjustable pillion footboards, a beneath-bike ground light for safer parking, an electrically activated reverse gear, and a touch-button electro-hydraulic center stand powerful enough to raise the bike fully loaded with rider, passenger, and luggage.

Tipping the scales at 387 kg (853 lbs) fueled, the K1200LT was 18 kg (40 lbs) lighter than the Gold Wing, with its monster six-cylinder, 1,832cc engine. The K1200LT was powered by a relatively modest, longitudinally aligned, 1,172cc in-line-four plant putting out 116hp (compared to 117hp for the Gold Wing). Its 120Nm (88lb-ft) of torque at 5,250rpm couldn't compete with the Honda's 171Nm (126lb-ft), but the K1200LT was significantly faster, with a top speed of 217 km/h (135 mph) to the Gold Wing's 200 km/h (124 mph).

Once you'd wrestled the K1200LT off the side-stand and let out the clutch, its handling belied its bulk and weight. All that torque made it relaxing to ride all day along unending highways (one complaint of many riders, however, was the five-speed gearbox's lack of an overdrive). Super-smooth acceleration powered it through corners and twisties like a sport bike. And BMW's signature Telelever front suspension and Paralever rear suspension (with preload adjustable spring) combined with a cast-aluminum single backbone with tubular-steel rear frame chassis to provide unflappable, sure-footed road-holding during aggressive riding. BMW's EVO servo-assisted braking and integral ABS were standard.

The K1200LT was sophisticated, reliable, and not least economical: it averaged 20 km/L (47 mpg). It wasn't cheap. But best yet for potential buyers, it was significantly cheaper than a Honda Gold Wing.

HP2 Enduro

Although the F650GS (introduced in 2000) and R1200GS adventure-touring models were highly capable off-road machines, BMW had yet to present true off-road enthusiasts with a dedicated, full-on enduro. In 2005, the enthusiasts' dreams came true. Inspired by the R900R (BMW's factory Paris-Dakar Rally bike) and the R1200GSA, the limited-production "high performance" HP2—the "2" references the twin cylinders of the boxer engine—was developed by a team of specialist engineers dedicated in their personal lives to off-road motorsport.

Although it used a similar 1,170cc engine as the R1200GS, this purist dirt bike boasted a mere 175 kg (386 lbs) dry weight—some 24 kg (53 lbs) lighter than the far bulkier, yet less-expensive GS sport tourer. The retuned engine and drivetrain were optimized for minimum weight and maximum off-road performance: for example, the balance shaft was removed (albeit at the inevitable cost of significant vibration). Power was boosted five horsepower to a claimed 105hp at 7,000rpm, while the HP2 motor produced 19Nm (14lb-ft) of torque more than the GS. This was huge heft for an enduro, but it was all smooth, controllable power that came on strong in all gears and gave a top speed of 200 km/h (125 mph).

The engine was set in an entirely new, lightweight steel-tube trellis spaceframe. Gone was BMW's trademark A-arm Telelever front suspension, replaced by a conventional upside-down telescopic fork with a massive 27cm (10.6ins) of travel. And the rear Paralever swingarm drive/suspension was 3cm (1.2ins) longer than on the GS; it also featured a unique adjustable compressed-air-damped shock that used neither spring nor oil—a first for mass-production motorcycles. Although armor-plated against rock hits below, the HP2 had no crash bars. However, two "salvaging bars" framing the headlight could be used to haul the bike out of deep mud and sand.

A truly uncompromising enduro, it came standard with outside-spoked wheels, tubeless Metzeler Karoo knobby dual-sport tires, and a 13-liter (3.4 gallons) fuel tank. A lower saddle, plus a tank-bag, small luggage-rack, and BMW's GPS navigation system, were options. The HP2 was never intended for touring, however, so hard panniers were never an option. Nonetheless, with road tires, it was a fun, high-performance urban ride. Off-road, its weight was a liability in boggy terrain. Otherwise, it handled supremely, and the year of its launch, a factory team tore a HP2 Enduro to third place in the ultra-challenging 1,685 km (1,047 miles) Baja 1000.

Production ceased in 2008. However, in 2007, BMW introduced the astronomically pricey HP2 Megamoto road bike using the same single overhead cam boxer engine. A third (and final) HP2 model—the Sport—launched in 2008 boasting BMW's first-ever dual overhead cam (DOHC) boxer motor, retuned to pour out 130bhp and to be purposefully aggressive and fast.

2005

R1200GS Adventure

With the introduction of the original R80G/S in 1980, BMW single-handedly created the adventure touring bike category. Thereafter it continually refined the big dual-sport model to be ever-more capable in any terrain. In 2006, the R1200GS Adventure set an entirely new standard. Many BMW aficionados consider it the *definitive* adventure model and the definitive motorcycle for global endurance riding.

The sibling R1200GS, introduced in 2004, was already considered the world's premier all-rounder bike, with virtually no scenario where it didn't excel. The new off-road-oriented Adventure upped the ante. One look told you this was a bike designed to handle everything Mother Nature could throw at it on long hauls over rugged terrain.

Most overt was its titanic 33-liter (8.7 gallons) fuel tank (giving a highway cruising range of up to 750 km [465 miles]), with crash guards for the fuel tank, hand-grips, and cylinder heads. The Adventure rode higher than the GS, with greater ground clearance, a 4.3cm (1.7in) taller adjustable seat, and longer suspension travel both front and back. It also had wider foot-pegs, a larger windscreen, and cross-spoked wheels with knobby tires. The bike had a formidable presence, especially when fitted with a full set of aluminum luggage. Only experienced riders (or the brave or foolish) would venture into nature's most daunting terrain on this giant. But on highways, the Adventure handled lightly and surely, with a broad, smooth power band that permitted all-day cruising at 160 km/h (100 mph).

2006

The Adventure got the latest generation 1,170cc mill, delivering 105hp at 7,500rpm and generating 120Nm (85lb-ft) of torque, same as the HP2 Megamoto. Both GS models shared a six-speed gearbox, but the Adventure got shorter gear ratios, including a 10-percent shorter first gear to facilitate technical creep-speed maneuvering through rocky terrain. The handlebars and foot brake lever were adjustable for stand-up riding off-road, while the ABS brakes could be switched off for better traction on sand and gravel. Optional extras included Automatic Stability control (ASC), Tire Pressure Control (TPC), and push-button Enduro Electronic Suspension Adjustment (ESA), which set up the chassis for variable loads and riding conditions. Plus, the Adventure's alternator put out 20 percent more watts than the standard GS, to accommodate the extra lights and electronic gadgetry adventure tourers were apt to add.

Factor in the bike's indefatigable reliability (not to mention heated grips and a trip computer), and the R1200GS Adventure was for two-wheel globetrotters the bike to own. It didn't hurt that actors Ewan McGregor and Charley Boorman, having solidified the R1150GS Adventure's reputation with their blockbuster *Long Way Round* TV series, used R1200GS Adventures for their *Long Way Down* sequel in 2007. Together, BMW's two GS bikes became the company's top-selling models, setting production records and requiring additional work shifts to meet worldwide demand.

F800GS

The sales success of the big-boxer GS models focused BMW's attention on the broader dual-sport market. The two 1,200cc machines were intimidatingly large for many riders. But BMW's equally popular mid-sized F650GS (which ceased production in 2007) was ripe for replacement, and especially for the addition of an Adventure variant. In model year 2008, the company presented its completely redeveloped, chain-driven, mid-sized F800GS enduro with liquid-cooled, in-line, parallel-twin 798cc engine.

The 75-horsepower motor was borrowed from the existing F800S and ST sport tourers but retuned—for example, with modified camshafts— for more even torque and greater power delivery at low- to mid-rpm, as desired for off-roading. It was mated to a six-speed transmission with broad gear ratios best suited to the bike's intended broad range of operating conditions.

2008

Set in a new trellis steel skeleton, the engine was canted forward 8.3 degrees (rather than 30 degrees, as in the F800S and ST). This freed up space for a wider radiator for more efficient cooling in low-gear, off-road terrain and a large 53cm (21in) front wheel without need for excessive rake. As with F series bikes since the early Funduro, the 16-liter (4.2 gallons) fuel tank was under the rider's seat; this lowered the bike's center of gravity and enabled a narrower physical profile. The faux-tank dummy hides twin air suction snorkels that aid high-river crossings.

Weighing about 22 kg (50 lbs) less than the R1200GS, the middle-weight F800GS was a far more capable off-road machine while also a strong urban and highway performer. This thanks, not least, to its compliant long-travel suspension (the double swingarm and preload-adjustable rear shock had more than 20cm [8in] of travel; the Marzocchi front forks offered a full 23cm [9in]) and comfortable upright ergonomics, including tapered handlebars and foot controls perfectly positioned for all-terrain riding. In short, it was a perfect weekday commuter and potent weekend adventure tourer.

As with the 1200GS, BMW introduced an even more robust F800GS Adventure with a larger underseat tank, extended crashbars, and a dream list of optional equipment (from auxiliary lighting, heated hand grips, and a lower seat to ABS brakes with turn-off switch) for tackling crossing continents. Both the F800GS and F800GS Adventure got ride-by-wire throttle control, with pre-programmed "Rain" and "Road" rider modes, plus optional "Enduro" and "Enduro Pro" modes for more demanding off-road use. Riding mode information was now displayed on the new, more easily readable, analog/LCD instrument panel.

As with its big boxer GS cousin, the F800GS proved a resounding sales success.

S1000RR

Introduced in April 2008, BMW's game-changing, race-oriented S1000RR sport bike was originally developed to compete in the 2009 Superbike World Championship. That year it entered commercial production, with an initial 1,000 made to satisfy World Superbike certification requirements.

Its ultra-short-stroke, 999cc engine was BMW Motorrad's first-ever transverse-mounted four-cylinder motor. It set a new standard for 1000cc series production Superbike technology. With a bore and stroke of 80mm × 49.7mm, it had the biggest bore in its class. Redlining at 14,200rpm, it was also the most powerful, pouring out 193 horsepower at 13,500rpm.

The S1000RR exemplified the German marque's pursuit of engineering excellence and technical innovation. For example, it was the world's first production motorcycle to offer a quick shifter (optional) for clutchless gear changes, even at full throttle. Borrowing from BMW's automotive division, it also introduced the motorcycle world to an optional electronic "dynamic traction control" (wed to a factory-fitted ABS system), which automatically curbed engine output and initiated other stabilization measures when loss of traction was detected. Plus, the S1000RR came standard with three riding modes (Wet, Sport, and Race).

Race-track-inspired R&D brought annual performance improvements. In 2012, for example, the chassis was upgraded: the wheelbase was reduced by 10mm (0.4in), the rear suspension was dropped 5mm (0.2 in), and the front lifted by a similar amount. For 2015, reshaped ports, a redesigned cam profile, lighter valves, shorter velocity stacks, and other modifications boosted output by 5.9 horsepower while shaving off 4 kgs (8.8 lbs) for a wet weight of 204 kg (450 lbs). And 2019 saw a complete model change, including an entirely new, 204-horsepower, 999cc engine that used only 5 percent of parts carried over from the earlier motor.

Some 11 kg (24 lbs) lighter, the 2019 motor employed BMW's patented ShiftCam technology—introduced on the same year's R1250GS boxer motor—with two different cam profiles that electronically varied the intake valve and cam lift timing, duration, and length according to desired optimum torque and performance. The hollow-bored intake valves and rocker arms were now made of lightweight titanium. And the water and oil pumps were combined into a single unit.

The S1000RR begat an even more powerful and subtly restyled version—the M1000RR—launched in 2022 and produced in parallel with the S bike.

K1600GT

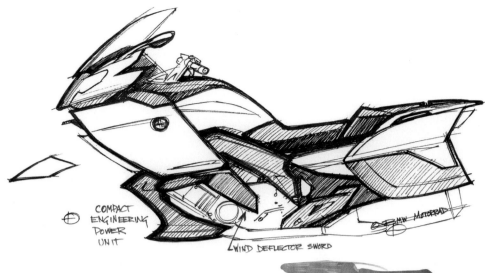

COMPACT
ENGINEERING
POWER
UNIT

WIND DEFLECTOR SWORD

2011

Above *An artistic rendering (left) for the blade-like K1600GT, and a 3D cutaway (right) showing its wishbone-style magnesium alloy main frame and light rear subframe.*

BMW's history is intimately associated with in-line six-cylinder engines, beginning in 1917 with Max Friz's seminal I-6 aircraft engine. In 1933, the company introduced the straight-six BMW 303 automobile, launching an association with automotive six-cylinder in-line engines that lasts to this day. For model year 2011, BMW introduced its first straight-six motor-cycles with the K1600GT and K1600GTL supersport tourers, unveiled at the International Motor Show in Cologne in October 2010. They were as sensational as the S1000RR and redefined the world's expectations for bikes in their class.

The spectacular K1600GT replaced the aging (and by now outdated and underpowered) K1200LT with a radical redesign centered around an all-new, liquid-cooled, 1,649cc in-line-six engine. Building upon the S100RR's space-packaging concepts, the 72mm cylinder bore was kept small, with a 67.5mm stroke and a mere 5 mm (0.2in) separating each cylinder, for an overall width of only 56cm (22in). Set transversely and til-ted forward 55 degrees, it was the motorcycle world's most compact and (at only 103 kg [227 lbs]) lightest straight-six production engine to date.

Producing 160 horsepower and 175Nm (129lb-ft) of torque, the silky-smooth, vibration-free powerplant had 12.2:1 compression and deli-vered massive linear thrust and top-end power. It could rocket from 0 to 100 km/h (62 mph) in three seconds and warped time with a top speed of 240 km/h (150mph).

As on the S1000RR, a touch-button control on the right-hand grip allowed the rider three engine output modes—Rain, Road, and Dynamic (for sporty riding)—via cylinder-specific adjustment to fuel injection using the latest ride-by-wire microelectronics. Optional Dynamic Traction Control (DTC) automatically optimized traction characteristics for each mode. The K1600GT also featured ABS and ESA (with predetermined settings for the Duolever front and Paralever rear suspension) as standard. The entire chassis and BMS-X engine management systems (not to mention the bike's state-of-the-art navigation and audio systems and even its variable-temperature, height-adjustable heated seat) could be controlled via a thumb-operated "Wonderwheel" Multi-Controller ring on the left handlebar.

A revolutionary carry-over from BMW automobiles was the K1600GT's gyro-controlled adaptive headlight, which constantly redirected the xenon beam to compensate for the bike's pitch and banking angle.

The K1600GT's blade-like aerodynamic profile suggested a dynamic ride. The lean-forward seating position was suitably aggressive. But long-distance comfort was also superb, thanks not least to a calm cockpit courtesy of the wind-tunnel-perfected adjustable windshield with memory function. Although physically massive, the bike's light, agile handling combined with phenomenal performance to set a new benchmark for high-performance sport touring bikes.

R1200RT

BMW first introduced an RT model in 1979 with the 980cc R100RT. Thirty-three years later, the comfortable, reliable, yet unpretentious tourer had evolved into a truly exciting sport tourer that combined practicality and reliability with truly mesmerizing performance and handling, not to mention sleeker eye-candy looks. Whereas the newly released K1600GT was now BMW's flagship tourer and stole some of the boxer-powered R1200RT's thunder, the latter was the purist's quintessential BMW tourer, fusing the latest mind-blowing technology with a dose of nostalgia to create a bike that was a pure joy to ride.

The original R1200RT, introduced in 2005 to replace the rather bland R1150RT, had an air/oil-cooled, 110-horsepower, 1,170cc SOHC motor. For model year 2010, it was significantly updated, using the HP2 Sport–derived DOHC valvetrain, new pistons, revised twin-spark plug boxer heads, and a servo-controlled valve in the two-into-one exhaust. It delivered the same horsepower but more torque, maxing at 119Nm (88lb-ft) and spread wider all the way to the higher 8,500rpm redline. This meant smoother delivery and more thrust at lower engine speeds.

The 2010 R1200RT also introduced BMW's Multi-Controller thumbwheel (beside the switchgear on the left handgrip), which controlled the optional audio system. (On the K1600GT, by comparison, it controlled everything from the GPS navigation to ESA.) The bike came with a wide range of optional accoutrements, such as heated handgrips and seats, onboard computer (fuel consumption, etc.), plus BMW/Garmin GPS navigation and a Bluetooth/iPod–compatible entertainment unit. BMW's ASC and ESA were also after-factory options.

Above left Design concept drawing for the R1200RT.

The 2014 model saw a sweeping redesign. Most importantly, it had a smoother running, air/water-cooled version of the 1,170cc boxer engine, now producing 125 horsepower. It came with Automatic Stability Control (ASC) plus two rider modes—"Rain" and "Road"—plus "Dynamic" riding mode with a "Hill Start Control Function" optional. The new R1200RT also had optional BMW Gear Shift Assistant Pro for clutchless upshifts and downshifts. Plus, it got the dynamic triple beam headlight introduced on the K1600 models. And its ergonomics were revamped, with the seat, handlebars, and footpegs all lowered for a more dynamic riding position.

This was a refined touring bike with excellent maneuverability. It loved winding roads, with plenty of clearance for aggressive leans through the bends. And optional cruise control (and a plush saddle) ensured effortless rides down long highways.

Given its potent performance and versatility, the R1200RT proved especially attractive to police around the world: BMW produced a law-enforcement version—the R1200FT-P—with programmable siren and LED emergency lighting, and rigged with mounts for everything from a radio intercom to a shotgun.

2012

HP4

2013

When introduced in 2009, the groundbreaking S1000RR was a technological tour de force, representing the zenith of BMW's engineering capabilities. It was hard to believe that the company would be able to improve upon its class-leading sport bike. Yet in 2012, BMW gave the S1000RR the "High Performance" treatment to create the track-oriented HP4 (released in 2013). This beautiful Bavarian bullet dripped with leading-edge electronics and race-inspired components never before seen outside MotoGP.

The lightest four-cylinder supersport bike in the 1,000cc class to date, the stock 193-horsepower machine came race-ready with a dry weight of just 169 kg (373 lbs)—fully 11 kg (25 lbs) less than the S1000RR. BMW also offered a 212-horsepower race-track version. It was noticeably more agile than the uber-agile S1000RR and could be flicked through corners with incomparable ease. Lightness aside, this was because the HP4 was also the most technologically advanced production sport bike yet built.

Not least, it introduced the motorcycle world to electronic Dynamic Damping Control (DDC). This adjusted the fork and shock rebound and compression damping every 11 milliseconds in response to road conditions. It worked in tandem with a Dynamic Traction Control (DTC) system featuring 15 different modes, including "Race" and "Slick" for the track: the latter featured a Launch Control setting to prevent wheelies off the line. The HP4 also introduced combined braking, which automatically applied the back brake in all modes except "Slick" when the rider applied the front brake.

The limited-production HP4 was made exclusively in 2013–2014. In 2017, BMW released the HP4 Race, a one-year-only, non-street-legal, track-only variant (cost: $78,000!) with a production run of 750 bikes. Fully fueled, it tipped the scales at a featherweight 171 kg (377 lbs). This thanks to its molded carbon-fiber monocoque frame, sub-frames, and wheels (30 percent lighter than the previous HP4's aluminum wheels), plus super-light titanium components, from the valves to the Akrapovič exhaust pipe and Brembo brake pistons. It was the world's first stock motorcycle with a fully carbon chassis and rims. Its hand-built, 999cc in-line-four engine poured out 215 horsepower at 13,900rpm. Crushing acceleration sent it to 193 km/h (120 mph) in second gear, with a top speed of 300 km/h (186 mph).

The carbon components improved the bike's ride dynamics. Despite carbon's extreme durability, BMW cautioned buyers that the HP4 Race motor was intended purely for the track and was built for only 5,000 kilometers (3,106 miles) duration before requiring a certified factory-built replacement engine!

F800GT

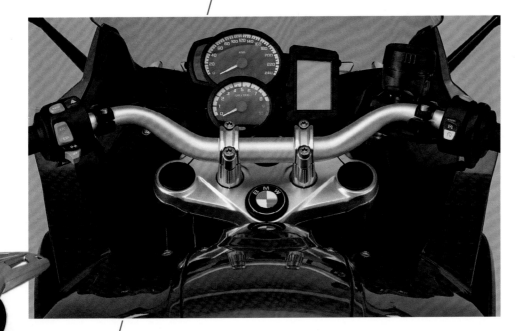

BMW hit a home run after partnering with Rotax, in Austria, to build a narrow, liquid-cooled 798cc parallel twin that powered the hugely successful midsize F800GS adventure model, launched in 2008. The motor had been developed to fill the yawning chasm between BMW's entry-level, single-cylinder F650s and large boxer twin R1200s, and was originally introduced in 2006 in the new F800S sport bike and F800ST sport tourer. Their size was ideal. But neither sold well. The S ceased production in 2010. For 2013, BMW revised the ST's platform and rebranded it as the F800GT light tourer.

The transverse, 12:1 compression powerplant retained its DOHC, four-valve-per-cylinder head and non-standard 360-degree firing order, with both pistons rising and falling together (the reciprocating action produced a somewhat boxer-like exhaust note, made raspier by a new, shorter silencer). But revised ignition and electronic fuel injection mapping bumped output 5 horsepower to 90hp. A swing-action balancing weight was employed to reduce vibration. Nonetheless, despite the counterbalance and newly rubber-mounted handgrips, riders complained of excessive buzz at high revs.

The ST's aluminum bridge-type frame was unchanged, but the GT got new ergonomics that improved rider comfort and handling. Higher grips and lower seat and footpegs (now farther forward) gave a more relaxed, upright position. Plus, a significantly longer single-sided rear-wheel swingarm, and shorter suspension at both ends, gave better road stability. The front fork remained non-adjustable. But the GT got Electronic Suspension Adjustment (ESA) that changed rear rebound damping, with "Comfort," "Normal," and "Sport" mode options. A sophisticated ABS system was standard for the triple disc brakes with Brembo four-piston calipers. And the optional Safety and Comfort packages added ESA, plus Automatic Stability Control (ASC) for optimized traction, an onboard computer, plus luggage bags and more.

The restyled GT had a far more aggressive profile than the S or ST, accentuated by its large camel-like tank hump (the actual 15-liter [4 gallons] fuel tank was under the seat) and a sharply defined yet taller, wider fairing and windshield. Lighter, restyled wheels helped improve the ST's already sharp cornering and handling. With huge torque and acceleration, a low center of gravity, and weighing only 213 kg (470 lbs) unladen, the F800GT was amazingly agile and easy to steer. BMW had finally brought its merely average middleweight ST up to par with the rest of the company's sport-touring lineup.

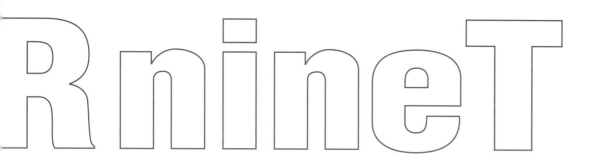

R nineT

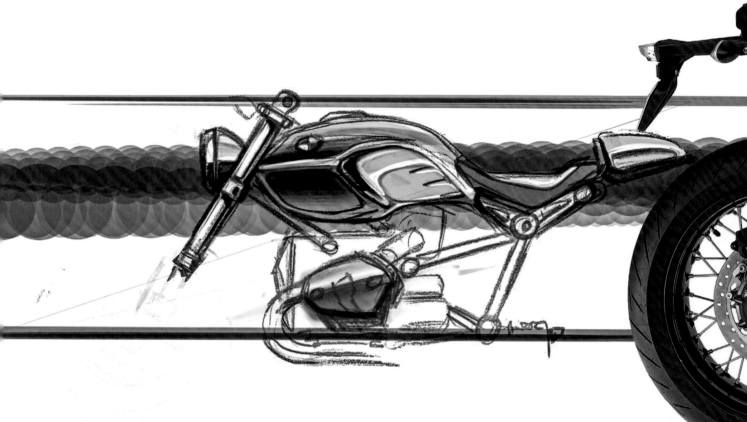

By 2013, BMW Motorrad had tapped almost every motorcycle market niche. In October, at the BMW Museum in Munich, it targeted two new markets by unveiling something totally unexpected: a classic retro-themed roadster—the R nineT—designed to celebrate nine decades of BMW motorcycles since the R32 in 1923. The first of BMW's new Heritage lineup, the minimalist roadster was initially intended to be the sole R nineT model. At its release, however, it had evolved to be a customizable café racer that appealed to BMW's youngest buying group ever. Four variants would soon follow. All got the same powerplant and cutting-edge technology.

BMW eschewed its latest water-cooled boxer engine and bolted the older air/oil-cooled 1,170cc twin as the central stressed member onto a tubular-steel spaceframe chassis, wed to the tried-and-true rear Paralever swingarm/shaft drive, but with a non-adjustable gold-anodized front upside-down fork. The same 110-horsepower oilhead engine that powered the original R1200GS bikes, its low-down torque and smooth power delivery made it the perfect motor for the R nineT in all its guises. It was paired to the GS/R/RT's six-speed transmission, but the drivetrain final drive ratio was slightly lower for quicker acceleration. The bike's fluted, double-barrel Akrapovič exhaust gave a sonorous, intoxicating burping bark.

The R nineT bore zero resemblance to the R32. But there was no denying its fantastic heritage looks, with design traits most closely resembling the /7 series.

Above left This conceptual drawing for the R nineT envisioned a retro-themed homage to the iconic R90 of 1973.

Its raw, stripped-back, yet elegant, aggressively modern-retro styling had massive character, heightened by a metallic black-painted aluminum 18-liter (4.8 gallons) gas tank, brushed at the knees. The right-side air scoop and sundry other parts were of clear-anodized aluminum.

The R nineT radiated raw power. Naked, it appeared ripe for customization; BMW offered countless personalization options, with four new models to work with. In 2016, it unveiled the less expensive, understated, back-to-basics R nineT Pure. Next year brought the more aggressive Racer with elongated chassis and café racer half-fairing (it was retired in 2019 due to poor sales). That year, BMW also introduced the R nineT Scrambler, with longer-travel suspension, a skid plate, raised exhaust, a 19-inch front wheel, and big knobby tires for light off-roading. And the 2017 Urban G/S was a soft-road-capable urban brawler painted in the blue-red-and-white color scheme of the original R80G/S model (for 2021, a one-year only "40 Years GS Edition" was offered in the black-and-yellow "bumblebee" colors of the R100GS for the anniversary of BMW's touring enduros).

For its 100th anniversary, BMW Motorrad announced a limited production—only 1,923 bikes—R nineT 100 Years edition with a chrome-plated/Black Storm Metallic tank and white double pinstriping in tribute to the 1969 R75/5.

2013

G310R/GS

Opposite *BMW and India's TVS Motor Company workers craft a clay prototype model of the G3IOR roadster.*

2016

The G310R—BMW's first budget, sub-300cc motorcycle—was intended as an entry-level naked roadster/sport bike to tempt beginner riders in Europe and North America, but it was presented around the globe as a premium compact bike for the broader market. Resembling a miniature S1000RR, the compact yet robust baby BMW was developed jointly with the TVS Motor Company of India. It was designed and engineered by BMW in Munich but built in India, overseen by BMW quality control staff.

The G310R is powered by a newly developed liquid-cooled, 313cc, single-cylinder engine with 80mm bore x 62.1mm stroke, producing 34 horsepower and 28Nm (21lb-ft) of torque. Its DOHC and four-valve configuration, Nikasil cylinder liner, and ultra-light rocker arms with DLC (Diamond Like Carbon) coating were based on the S1000RR superbike. The electronic fuel-injected powerplant has a backward-tilted cylinder reversed by 180 degrees, with the intake at the front and the exhaust to the back for more efficient airflow. This also permits the engine to sit closer to the front wheel for optimized weight distribution. A rotating counterbalance shaft in front of the crankshaft suppresses vibrations and ensures a smooth ride. Power is transmitted to the rear wheel via a constant-mesh six-speed gearbox.

The motor is mounted as a stressed member to a rigid, tubular, grid-structure steel frame with bolt-on rear frame. Offering precise steering, the bike's S1000RR-look-alike front end features non-adjustable, gold-anodized, upside-down forks and Bybre radial four-piston-caliper ABS brakes. The rear has an aluminum swingarm with single non-adjustable shock.

Tipping the scales at a mere 158.5 kg (349 lbs) unladen, the pocket-size G310R is as agile as a gazelle. Flat out, it couldcan just about reach "the ton" (161 km/h [100 mph]). A powerful, dynamic performer, it has lively pulling power, is easy to handle, and is equally at home on nimble urban commutes or blasting along twisting country roads.

In July 2018, BMW released the G310GS pint-sized adventure bike with gentler rake, longer wheelbase, longer-travel suspension, a preload-adjustable rear monoshock, and signature GS styling. Clad in dual-purpose tires, BMW's baby GS is good for dabbles in the dirt, such as fire roads, but lacks the potential for conquering rugged single-track trails.

Although budget Beemers priced for the value-conscious mainstream, both G310 models are well-built and boast a flawless finish. For 2021, they received Euro 5–compliant upgrades, including a new LED headlight, computerized ride-by-wire fuel injection, a slipper-assist clutch for silky gear-shifts, and low RPM-assist programmed to automatically increase revs if the engine is about to stall.

The big R1200GS dual-purpose BMW boxer inspiration is evident in the styling of the dirt-friendly G310GS.

K1600B

After debuting the K1600GT and GTL luxury tourer for 2012, BMW leveraged the platform's potential and released the K1600B—a "bagger" variant—for model year 2017. The new, large-displacement, high-performance, high-tech luxury touring bike was clearly aimed at the North American market. The K1600 had already established itself as the gold standard in touring. With its short-rise handlebar, tapered custom saddlebags, and lowered back end, the B cut a long, low-slung, streamlined, wave-like profile created with America's dimensions and landscape—not to mention comparable Milwaukee iron—in mind.

Its immensely powerful, silky-smooth, oil/liquid-cooled, 1,649cc, in-line-six engine fit the bill. The black-painted motor inclined forward 55 degrees to keep the bike's fully loaded 367 kg (809 lbs) mass down low. The B's entire sleek, lean-forward posture resembled a track star crouching eagerly at the blocks. And was it fast! Making 160 horsepower and 175Nm (129lb-ft) of torque, it delivered exhilarating FI-like acceleration previously unheard of for heavyweight tourers. The most powerful and fastest bike in its class, the "Blackstorm metal"-painted B left the equivalent (but merely 90-horsepower) Harley-Davidson Street Glide Special in the dust.

2017

It was electronic quickshifter–equipped and was loaded with all the bells and whistles, from cruise control and electronically adjustable windscreen to a plush heated seat, and even an electronic reverse gear (handy for getting out of tight parking spots), all standard. An optional Bagger Package included keyless/push-button engine start, anti-theft alarm, a twin-speaker Bluetooth-enabled stereo, a centerstand, and floorboards instead of pegs (riders complained that their feet felt the engine heat).

The B was upgraded in 2022 to be Euro 5–compliant. The triple-disc ABS braking now features six-axis IMU (inertial measuring unit) assist via smartphone-type chip that assesses the bike's lean, pitch, and yaw for optimized braking and to control the "Next Generation" Dynamic ESA. The IMU also powers a new drag torque control (MSR) that maintains sufficient revs to preserve traction during hard deceleration. Vehicle settings are now displayed on a huge (10.25in) liquid-crystal color screen with phone connectivity and integrated map navigation. And the BMS engine control now includes sensors to optimize ignition timing and exhaust emissions, while boosting torque and acceleration. However, all the new K1600s are now electronically limited: to 200 km/h (124 mph) for the B, and just 160 km/h (100 mph) for the luxurious Grand America—a full-dress variant elevated in 2022 from a former option package to a stand-alone model. The Grand America comes with a top-case and three exclusive paint and styling options, including Meteoric II Dust Metallic with a galaxy motif.

R1250GS
/GS Adventure

BMW's Swiss Army knife of motorcycles, the do-it-all, heavyweight GS and its rugged Adventure sibling, consistently account for one-third of BMW Motorrad's annual sales. That's one reason Harley-Davidson—*gasp!*—launched its 1,200cc Pan American adventure bike for model-year 2020. With Ducati, Honda, Kawasaki, KTM, Suzuki, Triumph, and Yamaha also at BMW's heels, the German marque continues to fine-tune its flagship models to stay ahead of the pack. In 2019, therefore, it released the R1250GS and GS Adventure, powered by a brand-new, air/liquid-cooled, 1,254cc boxer engine.

Compared to the previous R1200GS, the 84cc bigger motor amps up power by 13 horsepower and torque by 14 percent, thanks to BMW's impressively innovative ShiftCam technology. This electronically (and imperceptibly) switches between two distinct intake cam profiles to optimize valve timing and lift as revs and engine load shift in response to changes in throttle input. The result is improved combustion, better fuel economy, lower emissions, and mesmerizingly wide and far smoother power delivery, with bags of low-down torque—a phenomenal 108Nm (80lb-ft) right off idle at only 2,000rpm!

Although the chassis and suspension remain more or less the same, the revolutionary new powerband makes riding the R1250GS and GSA a far more exhilarating experience. Especially so when combined with BMW's now familiar Dynamic ESA. The new models also got Gear Shift Assist for drama-free clutchless shifts and "Dynamic," "Road," "Rain," and "Enduro" options in Ride Mode, each responsive to riding conditions with a unique combination of throttle response, peak power, plus DTC and ABS sensitivity settings. The Adventure also got an "Enduro Pro" setting: calibrated for off-road tires, it disables the linked braking and traction control to permit rear wheelspin and rear-brake lock-up for controlled slides.

Plus, the GS siblings got some new high-tech safety features. Dynamic Brake Control automatically closes the throttle during hard braking. And the Hill Start Pro function (with manual, automatic, and disable modes) automatically enables the brakes whenever the bike stops on an incline greater than five degrees; a twist of the throttle automatically releases the brakes.

Both models also got keyless ignition and LED adaptive swiveling headlights. And ex-works options include Intelligent Emergency Call summons assistance via an SOS button.

More sharp-angled than prior editions, with blacked-out engines, the new models are absolute stunners. The Triple Black edition has Darth Vader looks. The more subtle Style HP kit includes the BMW Motorsports red-white-and-blue paint scheme plus gold off-road-ready spoked wheels. The Adventure, with its longer travel suspension and large-capacity fuel tank, weighs 28 kg (40 lbs) more than its sibling. But otherwise, no prior generation of GS and GS Adventures has looked so alike—or appealing.

2019

R1250R/RS

The R1250GS and GS Adventure demonstrated that BMW's nearly one-century-old big-twin boxer engine has evolved to be a thunderously powerful and sporty, high-tech motor. When BMW introduced the naked R1250R roadster and faired R1250RS later in 2019, you could almost hear Q cautioning: "Now pay attention Bond. This new R1250RS is a lot racier than your last bike." Far more than simply roadgoing versions of the GS, the R and RS were now the most capable sport road motorcycles in their class.

Both bikes got the new-for-2019 1,254cc engine with ShiftCam technology delivering 134hp and a monstrous 142Nm (105lb-ft) of torque. Being lighter and leaner than the GSs, and with far taller gearing, they are faster—247 km/h (154 mph) top speed—and can rocket from 0 to 100 km/h (62 mph) in 2.9 seconds.

The bikes got most of the latest electronic safety aids being introduced across BMW's entire range. Among them, the Gearshift-Pro quickshifter, Hill Start Control set-off assist, and Automatic Stability Control (ASC) came standard. The R has 'Road' and 'Rain' rider modes, while a new ECO riding mode was added to the RS's quiver for maximum fuel efficiency. "Dynamic" and configurable "Dynamic Pro" were included within a Ridings Mode Pro optional package, which also added Dynamic Brake Control (DBC), Dynamic Traction Control (DTC), ABS Pro (cornering ABS), and Dynamic ESA "Next

The all-new R1250R (left) and racier R1250RS (right) flat-twins shared BMW's innovative silk-smooth ShiftCam, plus a choice of rider-aid packages.

Generation"—which now also control ABS levels—to automatically adjust suspension damping according to the riding mode selected.

A 6.5-inch full-color TFT dash displaying customizable navigation and vital vehicle information, plus music and phone connectivity functions, is now controlled via a thumbwheel Multi-Controller on the left grip, as on K1600 models.

The two models received a style refresh. The R got a large elliptical halogen headlight, while the RS dropped the wasp-like look of the S1000RR in favor of twin cat-eye LED lights. The minimalist R shunned bodywork for a raw roadster look, with a tiny flyscreen. Being more about long-range comfort, the RS is the yin to the R's yang, with a three-quarter front fairing and windscreen. Both got sporty-looking inverted front forks and an upswept subframe to loft the pillion seat high above the rear wheel. The mainframe with load-bearing engine was wed to the standard boxer single-side Paralever shaft/swingarm and monoshock.

The R and RS each offer an exhilarating ride that feels far different from that of the GS and GS Adventure. Stylistically, they are more distant cousins than siblings. More Japanese than Teutonic. Plus, their MSRP is below most of their Japanese competition.

2019

R18
/100Years

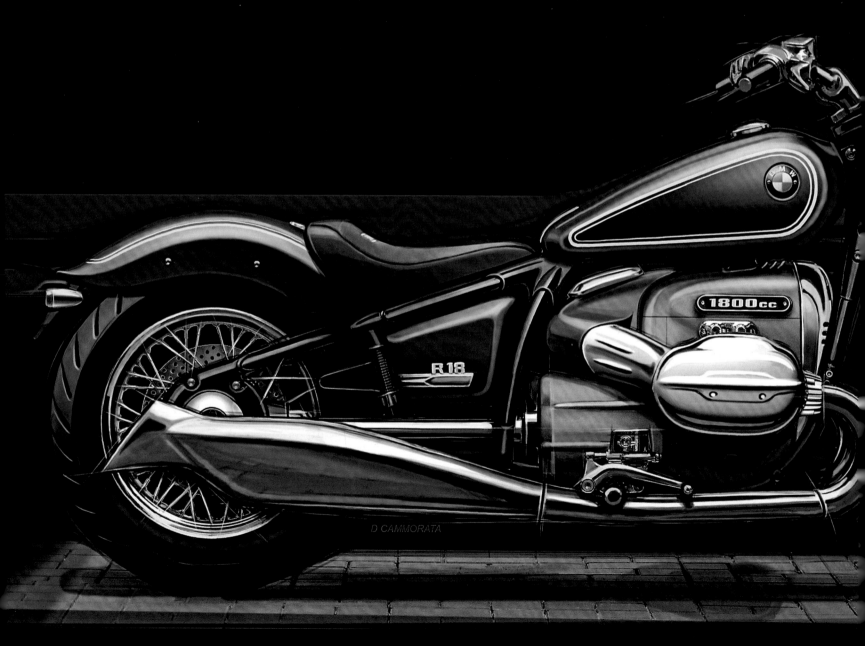

D CAMMORATA

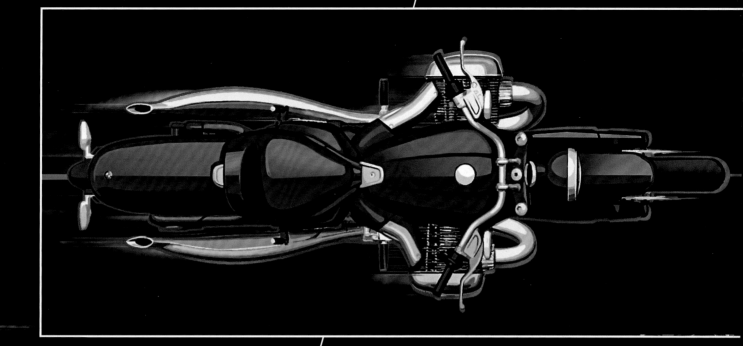

With the introduction in 2022 of the soulful R18, BMW Motorrad finally entered the distinctly American cruiser market long dominated by Harley-Davidson and Indian Motorcycle. BMW had taken a stab at the segment with its short-lived R1200C, built between 1997 and 2004. But the classically inspired R18 brought a whole new panache. BMW's second bike in its "Heritage" lineup, it has a stripped-down, stretched-out, raked-out, low-slung, purist look that borrows heavily from the iconic 1936 BMW R5.

There being no substitute for displacement in a heavyweight cruiser, the gloss black-painted R18 is powered by the highest capacity boxer engine ever produced. The new air-cooled, four-stroke, twin-cam, four-valve, flat-twin boxer motor has 9.6:1 compression, displaces 1,802cc (with a 107.1mm bore and 100mm stroke), and produces 91 horsepower and 157Nm (116lb-ft) of low-down torque, plentiful to move the bike's 345 kg (761 lbs) wet weight with ease. With mammoth deep-finned cylinders, the sparse boxer engine—appearing comically large in its "hardtail" double-cradle steel-tube frame—is the epicenter of the flashback R18 persona. The engine features old-fashioned pushrods (even the original R5 used state-of-the-art chain-driven cams). Gorgeous twin fishtail exhausts are R5-inspired. And in lieu of BMW's standard Paralever, its nickel-plated driveshaft (connected to a cantilevered monoshock rear end) is exposed, just like the R5.

Above The chrome-clad R18 100 Years reflected a dazzling century of motorcycle production. Each of the 1,923 limited-edition bikes got a unique numbered badge atop the tank.

Right Clean. Minimalist. Suave. The magnificent retro-themed R18 100 Years is truly one for the ages.

While the R18 boasts electronic fuel injection and BMS electronic engine management, BMW dispensed with most electronic adjustment options, including for the suspension. An optional premium package, however, includes adaptive headlights, heated grips, Hill Start Control assist, an electronically activated reverse gear, plus Active Cruise Control (ACC), which automatically reduces the bike's speed if it detects a vehicle too close ahead.

Within a year, the R18 family grew to four members. First came the R18 Classic, with a windshield and semi-soft saddlebags. For 2022, BMW added the R18B "bagger," with a blacked-out engine, streamlined hard cases, a fork-mounted full fairing (non-adjustable), and a full infotainment system, and the fully dressed, flagship R18 Transcontinental, which also has a top trunk with wraparound passenger backrest. The 429 kg (941 lbs) Transcontinental also got a sturdier frame, shorter wheelbase, larger front wheel and gas tank, and BMW's proprietary Multi-Controller wheel and the latest 10.25-inch TFT infographic display.

For 2023, a limited edition R18 100 Years model of just 1,923 bikes celebrated BMW's centenary. Harking back decades, its black tear-drop tank and rear fender got a sophisticated paint-on-chrome treatment with white double-pinstriping. The engine case, cylinders, and rear drive are painted black. A surfeit of chrome includes the engine cover, cylinder head covers, intake manifold covers, and Akrapovič mufflers with perforated BMW logos at their tips. And the two-toned black solo seat is embossed with a diamond pattern in oxblood red.

M1000RR
/50YearsM

Riders for whom the sizzling S1000RR's performance simply wasn't enough were surely grinning when BMW Motorrad released the higher-spec, competition-focused but still road legal M1000RR variant in September 2020. Aimed at club racers, track-day connoisseurs, and well-heeled speed freaks, its main purpose is for BMW Motorsport GmbH engineers to evolve a World Superbike championship winner. The uber-performing M1000RR—the first motorcycle with the "M" prefix normally associated with BMW's high-performance cars—is a homologation special fitted with street-spec equipment to meet legal requirements for road use and World Superbike regulations for production-based racing.

At a glance, the S1000RR and M1000RR (which is uniquely adorned with the circular BMW 'M' brand logo) look like identical twins. BMW's engineers used the S1000RR's water-cooled, 998cc, in-line four-cylinder powerplant with ShiftCam technology and tweaked it to boost horsepower from 206.6hp to 212hp at 14,500rpm thanks to a revised 13.5 compression combustion chamber; lighter, lower-friction two-ring forged Mahle pistons; lightweight titanium valves and connecting rods; and a titanium Akrapovič exhaust that shaved 3.6 kg (8 lbs) off the S1000RR's system. Maximum torque remained at the S1000RR's 113Nm (83.3lb-ft) at 11,000rpm, with a new 15,100rpm redline (500rpm higher than the S model).

The M1000RR was also aerodynamically redesigned in a wind tunnel. The optimized carbon fairing and upside-down Marzocchi front fork sprouted downforce-producing winglets to increase traction, especially in high-lean corners. And new carbon-fiber front-wheel guards got special brake ducts that reduce turbulence around the new carbon wheel.

The result? An insanely quick racer that, for the brave at heart, manages to also be a flexible and super-sporty country-road bike, thanks to such features as Launch Control and a Pit Lane Limiter that knows when to automatically curb power.

To mark the 50th anniversary of BMW Motorsport GmbH, in May 2022, BMW Motorrad presented a special edition M1000RR 50 Years M model, available for six months only. Painted in striking Sao Paulo Yellow, it was fitted with the (normally) optional M Carbon and M Competition Packages as standard. Tantalizing accoutrements included a lighter anodized aluminum swingarm, additional carbon-fiber parts, an endurance chain, special brake and clutch levers, a pillion package, and activation for the GPS Lap Timer and data logger app.

With its blistering top speed of 314 km/h (195 mph), the M1000RR has since 2021 served as the base bike for the BMW Motorrad World Superbike team. It seems remarkable that this engineering masterpiece can be purchased by the general public. Unrivaled performance and exclusivity are guaranteed—for twice the price of the S1000RR!

The M1000RR 50 Years M: Almost 100 years of motorcycle racing spirit and 50 years of motorsport history combined in one exclusive bike.

THE AUTHOR

CHRISTOPHER P. BAKER has been a successful travel writer, photographer, and motor-journalist for more than four decades. His feature articles on motorcycles and motorcycle touring have appeared in *Adventure Motorcycle Rider*, *Bike*, *BMW Motorcycle Magazine*, *CNN*, *Motorcyclist*, *National Geographic Traveler*, *Ride*, *Rider*, and *Travel + Leisure*, among others. Baker has also authored more than 30 books, including *Harley-Davidsons: Engines and Evolution* and *Mi Moto Fidel: Motorcycling Through Castro's Cuba*—winner of the Lowell Thomas Award "Travel Book of the Year" and NATJA Grand Prize. He arranges and leads group motorcycle tours of Cuba by BMW F800GS. He lives in California, where he rides a BMW R1200GSA.

Project editor
Valeria Manferto De Fabianis

Editorial assistant
Giorgio Ferrero

Graphic design
Paola Piacco

WS White Star Publishers® is a registered trademark property of White Star s.r.l.

© 2023 White Star s.r.l.
Piazzale Luigi Cadorna, 6 - 20123 Milan, Italy
www.whitestar.it

Editing: Abby Young

ISBN 978-88-544-2003-8
1 2 3 4 5 6   27 26 25 24 23

Printed in China